Sacred MONEY

The POWER of Heart-Centered Finance

Genevieve Chavez Mitchell

Sacred Money
The Power of Heart-Centered Finance

In this world of digital information and rapidly-changing technology, some citations do not provide exact page numbers or credit the original source. We regret any errors, which are a result of the ease with which we consume information.

Excerpted from *The Circle of Life* by Joyce Rupp and Macrina Wiederkehr, ©2005. Used with permission of the publisher, Sorin Books®, an imprint of Ave Maria Press®, Inc., P.O. Box 428, Notre Dame, IN 46556, www.sorinbooks.com.

Disclaimer: Genevieve Chavez Mitchell is not a financial professional and the contents of this book are for educational purposes and do not constitute financial or investment advice.

All stories, clients, and individuals cited in this book are real. Most of the names, situations, and locations have been changed. Thank you to those who agreed to share their names and stories.

Edited by Anna Paradox
Cover Design by: Kristina Edstrom
Mandala Art by: Maryanne Carter
Author photo by: Angie Chavez

An Imprint for GracePoint Publishing (www.GracePointPublishing.com)

GracePoint Matrix, LLC
624 S. Cascade Ave, Suite 201, Colorado Springs, CO 80903
www.GracePointMatrix.com Email: Admin@GracePointMatrix.com
SAN # 991-6032

A Library of Congress Control Number has been requested and is pending.

ISBN: (Paperback) 978-1-961347-19-9
eISBN: 978-1-961347-18-2

Books may be purchased for educational, business, or sales promotional use.
For bulk order requests and price schedule contact:
Orders@GracePointPublishing.com

For my grandchildren, Eliora, Caleb, Alice, Jude, and all new babies on the way. May the world you inhabit be just, kind, and sustainable. May you always recognize your Divinity and your connection to Mother Earth.

Praise for *Sacred Money*

Genevieve's book is a gift! Her focus on women and money is practical, insightful and generous. Combining heart and mind in its approach, *Sacred Money* begins to close the financial knowledge gap by offering a path forward for getting out of debt and building wealth, something women and girls need now more than ever.

Giovanna Rossi, MSc
Women's Health and Rights Consultant, Trainer and Coach
Producer/Host, The Well Woman Show on NPR

Money can be life-giving if shared. Genevieve Chavez Mitchell invites the reader to explore their money story with an eye toward socially and ecologically enhancing investment. Exercises, rituals, and affirmations foster community-focused consumption and global well-being. This is helpful guide to an economically conscious spirituality.

Diann L. Neu
Cofounder and Codirector of
Women's Alliance for Theology, Ethics and Ritual

Too many sincere, hardworking people—especially women—still struggle to find a soulful, comprehensive approach to money. Well, here is a powerful and refreshing answer from Genevieve Chavez Mitchell in *Sacred Money!* She shows us step-by-step how to discover our vision, align with our ethical values, and take practical actions—all with her loving 'I'm your big sister right beside you' vibe. This book is a masterpiece of emotional intimacy and financial practicality.

Rev. Karen Russo, MBA
award-winning author, *The Money Keys:*
Unlocking Peace, Freedom, and Real Financial Power

Genevieve Chavez Mitchell doesn't just offer a book; she gives a precious treasure—a blueprint for resurrecting our cold, lifeless relationship with money. With her masterful storytelling, purposeful exercises, and profound insights, she expertly guides us toward reconciling our financial lives with our deepest values and spiritual beliefs. Then, she unveils the transformative nature of deliberate financial choices, empowering us to catalyze positive change in the world. No matter your wealth, from monk-like simplicity to tech founder lavishness, this book comes highly recommended!

Paul Zelizer
Social Entrepreneur Coach and
Impact Investing Evangelist

Sacred money? Heart-centered finances? Yes and thank you! Genevieve presents a wholistic, balanced approach to understanding our personal relationships with money by offering focused intentions and rituals to open new doorways to the whole mystery that money can be. Her personal stories could be from any of us as we acknowledge our ingrained patterns of money and finance, especially as women who, traditionally, are vulnerable to the male-dominated world of money, investment, and power. She also delves into new ways of how to use money for bigger, world-related benefits that can be life changing for people and our planet. Bringing money in as a sacred tool is life changing. Genevieve's vision and dedication have created a powerful tool in this book.

Kathryn Ravenwood
Author of *How To Create Sacred Water:*
A Guide to Rituals and Practices

Sacred Money: The Power of Heart-Centered Finance by Genevieve Chavez Mitchell is a must read. It's a beautiful balance of personal stories, rituals, spiritual practices, and education. All shared while never losing sight of the bigger picture of "blend[ing] the world of money and investing with our inner sacred selves." Genevieve provides the vision; the steps; and the activities to help you heal your money story and incorporate mindful changes into your own life. She also shares with readers the vision of transforming the financial system to move towards a more collective and conscious mindset. This book is provocative; healing; and reinforcing…all while providing concrete strategies to make sustainable changes.

Barbra Portzline, Ph.D.
Founder, Organizational Rebel® LLC

Both a quest and a roadmap, this book provides both a smart guidepost and deep challenges. Genevieve Chavez Mitchell opens her heart, sharing her personal experiences to help the reader find the courage—and wisdom—to move forward. This book broaches a subject often eschewed by spiritual seekers—how do we align our spiritual and material selves? The questions, rituals, affirmations, and journal prompts give us a way forward.

Anne Key
Founder, Goddess Ink Publishing

In a world where money is often seen as the ultimate measure of success and happiness, it's refreshing to read a book that challenges this conventional wisdom. In *Sacred Money: The Power of Heart-Centered Finance*, author Genevieve Chavez Mitchell invites us to reconsider our relationship with money and to embrace a new paradigm that is based on values such as cooperation, sustainability, and social justice.

The author begins by exploring our obsession with materialism and consumerism and how this is leading to a number of serious problems, including environmental destruction, social inequality, and a growing sense of alienation. She encourages shifting our money mindset to recognize it as a tool, not a goal, and used to support our values and to create a more just and sustainable world.

Chavez Mitchell also discusses the role of women in the new money paradigm. She argues that women have a unique perspective on money and that they are uniquely positioned to lead the way in creating a more just and sustainable financial system.

Sacred Money: The Power of Heart-Centered Finance is a thought-provoking and inspiring book that challenges us to rethink our relationship with money. It is a must-read for women who are interested in a wholistic approach to money, creating a more just and sustainable world.

Overall Rating: 5/5 stars

Brenda Billings Ridgley
Author of Lady and the Tribe:
How to Create Empowering Friendship Circles.

There are many books on money and money management, but never has there been a book quite like *Sacred Money* that balances the practical and the spiritual so seamlessly. Chavez Mitchell has written an extraordinary book especially but not only for women–a book that grasps the deeper implications, ramifications, and consequences of money on our lives and relationship with the world, balances practical guidance with empowering affirmations and prayers, and is full of heart, wisdom, and vision for humanity. Understanding the urgency of moving from a "Me, More, Mine" paradigm to one that invests in humanity and the Earth, Chavez Mitchell has walked her talk, investing in her neighbors and community to move people out of debt and out of stuck patterns with money into a grace filled, sacred, complete, and whole life. It took a strong, mature, and fully conscious, loving woman to write this gem of a book—and Chavez Mitchell brings the wealth of her life experience to this labor of love. Indeed, the birth of this book feels like a sacred gift. In an era of mounting ecological crises and global insecurity, Chavez Mitchell brings a timely and healing message that deserves wide readership in book clubs and homes across the land.

Glenn Aparicio Parry
Two-time Nautilus award winning author of
Original Thinking: A Radical ReVisioning of Time, Humanity and Nature and
Original Politics: Making America Sacred Again.

In a time of so much separation, *Sacred Money* is a great read to remind us of the infinite possibilities to recognize that individually we can make an impact through our money choices. This book offers exercises for immediate change. It is filled with actionable insights you can take and put into place today to make an impact. Genevieve Chavez Mitchell has opened the door to a better conversation to help you and your community through conscious money choices.

Susan Davis, ThM
Author of *Creating Life Balance: Strategies to Thrive*

Organized around the turn of the seasons and full of rituals, sacred practices, and practical money management advice, this book is like no other financial book available, weaving together magic and intention, dollars and sense, into one supportive, nourishing, and heart-centered guidebook to living your values, while making a living at the same time. It does not ignore collective well-being or our responsibility to one another and the planet, as it explores issues of consumption as well as the joy of creation. *Sacred Money* is an amazingly unique, and needed, contribution to both financial and spiritual understanding and thriving.

Molly Remer
author of *Womanrunes, Walking with Persephone*, and
365 Days of Goddess, creatrix of the
#30DaysofGoddess devotional practice.

In her book *Sacred Money*, Genevieve Chavez Mitchell takes the reader on a seasonal journey full of insights to help them awaken their connection to the sacredness of money. She gently weaves personal stories, community caring, reader exercises, and global possibilities, into this gem of a book in a way that brings hope for our collective financial future.

Lisa Michaels
Author and Visionary Nature Aligned Leadership Mentor

It is deeply refreshing to find a grounded, practical, and integrative approach to building a healthy relationship with money. *Sacred Money* provides both spiritual grounding and tactical advice. A must read for conscious entrepreneurs!

Pamela Slim
author, *Body of Work* and *The Widest Net*

Genevieve Chavez Mitchell's *Sacred Money, The Power of Heart-Centered Finance* is a masterful and evocative journey through the mystery of money as an embodiment of the feminine divine principles of reciprocity and flow. Mitchell masterfully weaves financial literacy with her authentic experiences and profound insights, guiding readers to explore their own complex relationships with money and the human experience. Mitchell navigates the intricacies of suppressed beliefs and fears with the grace of a priestess, inviting readers to explore the transformative power of rituals. Highly recommended for anyone seeking a transformative experience that harmonizes personal finance with our interconnected world.

Dr. Patricia Klauer
Technology and Consciousness Leader

Table of Contents

Foreword

Our world is not heading in the right direction. If we are to change the trajectory of our species, we must leverage our two most potent tools: consciousness and capital. Genevieve Chavez Mitchell's ground-breaking book, *Sacred Money: The Power of Heart-Centered Finance*, serves as a clarion call for this vital transformation.

Genevieve doesn't just invite you on a journey, she beckons you toward a revolution—one that redefines your relationship with money and, by extension, the world. This book is more than a guide, it's a manifesto for creating a more compassionate and equitable world. As I delved into its pages, I felt a seismic shift in perspective, one that has the power to ignite change in anyone willing to absorb its teachings.

My life's mission, articulated in my own book, *The Secrets of the Season: You're Here For a Reason*, aligns seamlessly with Genevieve's vision. Through our collective work with conscious capital, we aim to transform the very fabric of society. Genevieve's book is a pivotal addition to this mission, offering actionable steps to wield money as an instrument of positive change in these critical times.

Shamans remind us that we dream our world into being. *Sacred Money* empowers us to dream anew. It challenges the status quo, urging us to see money as a sacred tool for both personal and planetary betterment. Genevieve dismantles the greed-driven paradigms that have led us astray, offering instead a vision that encompasses the well-being of all life forms and the planet itself.

Genevieve doesn't just preach, she provides a toolkit for transformation. From practical exercises to soul-stirring affirmations, she offers a pathway to align financial life with ethical stewardship and genuine generosity. This book is a roadmap for transcending the limiting narratives that cloud our understanding of true wealth.

I've had the privilege of knowing Genevieve for years and can attest to her unique blend of spiritual wisdom and financial acumen. Her extensive experience in facilitating personal and business growth loans, coupled with her active involvement in transformative organizations like Future Capital and Invest for Better, makes her an authoritative voice in the realm of conscious finance.

Sacred Money is not just a book, it's a movement. It's a catalyst for reimagining a world where the currencies of love and financial capital harmoniously coexist. I urge you to embrace this transformative power of heart-centered finance. Let it be the change you wish to see—one heart, one dream, one revolution at a time.

Lawrence Ford, CEO, CCO
Conscious Capital Wealth Management, LLC,
Shaman of Wall Street

Part One
Welcome

Introduction: You Can Change the World

It's time to heal the divide between money and your sacred self. If you want to use your money and your best self to help create a world that works for all, you can. This book is for those who want to improve their relationship with money and acknowledge the power and sacredness of the Divine.

Our society separates the inner, spiritual self and the outward world of money, economics, and finances. I've felt the conflict between my spiritual self and my finances. The temple or the church used to be the tallest building in town; now it's the bank. The market is on one side of the street and the temple is on the other. It's time to end that division and connect our hearts and our material well-being.

Money is a given in our world. It can be wonderful, and it can be challenging. It also can be a powerful tool for social change and transforming our economy.

Like you, I have struggled with making money, having money, not having money, spending money, not spending money. I have been selfish, greedy, judgmental, and self-centered. I have wanted money, worked for money, lost money, wasted money, fought about money, worried about money, and cried about money. There have also been times when I've been generous, thoughtful, and helpful with others using my money. It's a path and a process, not an exact science. I'm still trying to get it right, but I will share a bit of what I have discovered in this book.

I am a spiritual being; you are a spiritual being. Our spiritual life is so rich, so substantial, so abundant and so profound—it's the mystery of life! Using our money, our resources, and our commitment to the Earth, we can bring this spiritual connection to our finances, and to our choices to help create a new world—a just, kind, regenerative world, for ourselves and future generations.

When I talk about spirituality, I mean the life force, a fully alive connection to meaning, purpose, and innate divine nature. You are a holy being, a soul; you have and are a divine presence manifesting as a human being in the here and now. You are sacred, just as you are.

I'm writing this book as a priestess. I walk on this Earth honoring the Sacred in who I am and in who you are. For me, this inner self is foundational and fundamental. It's the lens through which I view the world.

We will walk together through our seasons of money, life, and spirit. We will use the seasons of the year as a framework for transforming our relationship with our money. Winter (surrender, silence, and darkness), spring (light returning, cultivation, and planting seeds), summer (growth, gifts, and green), and autumn (harvest, gratefulness, and sharing) each bring ways to connect our money to nature, seasons, and cycles of life. These seasons of money, Winter, Spring, Summer, and Autumn, differ as much as the actual seasons of the year, and we will explore each in depth.

You may decide to make this journey by yourself, with another person, or in a group. Having support helps us stay on the journey.

A journey isn't so much about walking the straight path, but rather finding the beauty and magic along the tangled, crooked road to using money in new ways. You can find a new way to be in a relationship with money. You can create a new framework for money. The old model of greed, accumulation, and plunder of Earth's resources needs to change. It's time to connect to our sacred self and find ways to use money to create a more just, sustainable Earth.

Let's walk in pilgrimage together, as companions on a sacred odyssey. Let's create a new paradigm about the role of finance in the world. Let's build a healthy relationship with money, and let's find innovative ways to use our resources to create a just, kind, sustainable world.

There are many stories included in this book, and all the stories are true. These stories come from clients, classes, meetings, and conversations with friends and colleagues. I have changed names and identifying information, but the heart of the story is true. I share my personal stories from my perspective and my point of view.

During our time together, we will be using a variety of tools (see chapter 2 on Preparation and Tools for the Journey). One tool we will use throughout the book is affirmations. These sweet notes to yourself can be used as inspiration or as a prompt. You can put them in your calendar or use them as a reminder of your financial commitment to yourself.

Affirmations

- I am at peace with money.
- I am so pleased to take this time with myself and my money.
- I have all the Divine guidance and support I need for this journey.

Chapter 1
The Day My World Changed

Owning our story and loving ourselves through that process is the bravest thing that we will ever do.
—Brené Brown

Each of us has a money story, a narrative that we have told ourselves and told to others. Society frequently tells us we only have value by what we own or how much we produce.

Many of us grew up not feeling valued or accepted for who we were as people. One of my realizations is that when I was younger, I knew what I did had value (doing my chores, raising children, feeding my family, volunteering), but I don't think that I personally had value. That was a societal story I had been told: Women didn't have value. I accepted that as the truth. At this stage of my life, I am recognizing and realizing that each of us has intrinsic value, an inherent, innate grace of God/Goddess Divine worth. I also recognize that I need to value myself and not expect others to provide acceptance, acknowledgment, or recognition for me to feel good about myself. Rather, it's up to me to provide approval and appreciation to myself, for being me. You and I have inherent worth because we are Divine creations.

Years ago, at the request of a friend who needed help with credit card debt, my husband, Paul, and I loaned her the money to consolidate her credit card debt, and after a time, become debt free.[1] Over time, we started doing small person-to-person and small business loans to help people who wouldn't otherwise qualify for a loan. Over the past twenty years, we have helped people with credit card debt, mortgage issues, business expansion, new technology, farm expansion, and real estate development. During those years, we have loaned money, given money, lost money, made money, and stressed over money. Behind all those decisions and exchanges is a deep recognition that I am a steward of money and resources. I am inextricably linked to people and the planet because I see myself as a global citizen. The gifts, talents, and resources I have are not just for my personal use, but rather, they are to be used for the benefit of the whole.

This is not something that has come easily or quickly, and it is a perspective that I continue to refine. I have made many money mistakes. Disagreements and conflicts about money were once part of my life. I accepted those conflicts as a normal part of life. Unfortunately, I also blamed myself for my lack of knowledge, understanding, and expertise about money. I thought my money issues were my fault because I was not "doing it right." I spent many years feeling like a failure about money. It seemed I could never do it right. What I realize is there is no "right way." We engage our money the way we engage our life, doing the best we can.

For years, I gave our money decisions to my husband. Yes, I kept a very frugal household account, but the rest, I handed over to my very smart, CPA (certified public accountant) partner. It was easy. He has an accounting degree, he is a CPA, he knows the business, and he counsels people about money, taxes, and estate planning. He's the expert, right? So, I said to him, "Here you go. You take care of the money." It was simple. It didn't require any effort on my part because I didn't take any responsibility for our financial decisions. Even when he asked me to participate, or engaged me in a discussion, I hesitated, agreed with his observations, or refused to be brought into the conversation. I avoided money discussions; they were just too painful. I had feelings of frustration, resentment, and disappointment in myself. I simply didn't know enough about our money to help or participate in our money decisions. In addition, I felt like I didn't have access to our money, because I didn't know how to pay attention, or how to participate in the ongoing process of our fiscal responsibility. I left it up to my very kind, very patient husband because that's what I had been taught to do: Leave money to the man of the house.

Over time, I came to appreciate that I had responsibility as a steward of our resources. I wanted my money—our money—to go toward a just, sustainable world. So, I began my journey to learn about money management and investing. It's been a process of looking at myself and how I viewed money and my beliefs about money. It is an ongoing process because money is a constant companion in our life and work. It's a journey, one that requires care, tending, planning, decisions, and awareness.

Finding this framework had a profound and lasting impact on my life. It happened on a cold January day back in 1991. Paul, my husband of five years, and I were the parents of four very young boys. Our oldest son, Luke, was almost four years old. Aaron had recently turned three, our third son, Jacob, was almost two, and our baby, Adam, was four months old. Yes, I had my hands full.

We lived in the desert of southern New Mexico, just outside of New Mexico's second-largest city of Las Cruces. Our little house, built in the 1940s, sat on an acre of land with a mature pecan orchard. The weather was mostly dry, sunny, and warm; it rarely snowed. Since I am married to a CPA, tax season was a very real event at our home. We made a point to take the kids to play in the snow in January before tax season started; there was no playtime with Daddy come mid-January.

That year, we loaded up the kids in my 1985 gray minivan with four car seats, plenty of warm clothes, and enough food for the weekend. We drove the two hours east, up the hill to the small mountain town of Cloudcroft. There was snow on the mountain, and the boys were excited we were going sledding. We rented a small cottage up the hill from Main Street. Beautiful, white snow covered the ground, and pine trees towered over the cabin.

Saturday morning, we drove up the mountain to a local favorite spot for inner tubing and sledding. As it rarely snows in our southern New Mexico desert, being in the snowy mountains was a treat! Sunday morning, we decided that Paul would take the big boys (Luke and Aaron, both age three) and I would keep nineteen-month-old Jacob and baby Adam and attend mass at a chapel a short walk down the hill.

Mid-morning Sunday, I dressed warmly and bundled up my little ones. I put Jacob in the backpack and Adam in the snuggly and headed out the door. It was a slow downhill walk in the snow with two babies. But it was important for me to get to mass. My commitment to weekly church was part of what held my life together. I was a "good Catholic girl." I followed church teachings, I accepted the dogma, I faithfully attended church, and I followed the rules of the Roman Catholic Church, without question. The Church has very defined roles for women, mostly following the biblical admonition to be a faithful helpmate to the husband, subservient, and submissive to all church teachings. All of that was about to change.

The church was a small chapel, built on a rocky hillside. Outside was a small sign, Mass: Sunday, 10 a.m. I walked in and found a seat near the back of the church. I took off the backpack and sat Jacob on the pew next to me. I unwrapped the snuggly and laid Adam on my black warm winter coat. Then I took off baby coats, hats, and scarves as other parishioners ambled in the front door.

At 10:00 a.m., the congregation opened with a song. Out from the sacristy came a WOMAN! Completely dressed in priestly vestments—a clerical collar, a white alb, a cassock, and a lovely, colorful handmade liturgical stole. I was stunned. I really didn't know quite what to do. Should I leave? Should I stay? This obviously was NOT a Roman Catholic Church.

In those days, religions didn't cross, and I had never seen the inside of anything but a Catholic Church. But here I was, with a woman, celebrating traditional mass. My whole self was shaken inside. Here was a female, proclaiming the gospel, consecrating the Eucharist, and blessing the congregation. A woman, in a powerful and important role as leader of this tiny church community in this tiny town in New Mexico—here was A WOMAN in SPIRITUAL LEADERSHIP!

In truth, I had never seen a woman in spiritual leadership. I had been around nuns as teachers of catechism. I knew nuns as caretakers of the church that I attended as a child. I knew one sister who started a food pantry where I volunteered time bagging groceries for hungry families. But, never, in my thirty-four years, had I seen a woman leading a worship service. It was a profoundly moving and intensely disruptive experience. It truly was *The Day My World Changed!*

I had walked into an Episcopal church, which had begun ordaining women in 1974. Sixteen years after the first women priests were ordained in Philadelphia, I walked into this small chapel and walked out a changed woman.[2] Something shifted in me. There was a light coming through to shine on a new way to see womanhood. I was jolted awake to my own inner divinity by seeing another woman share her spiritual guidance and leadership with me. I had no way of knowing where this new way of thinking would lead me, but I was forever changed.

Years later, I was at a Call-to-Action Catholic Reform meeting. A woman shared a story of going to Japan with her American-born,

Japanese husband. They walked into a church in Tokyo where an image of a Japanese Christ hung on the cross. Her husband was deeply moved and began crying. He turned to her and said, "I can now see myself in Jesus." That story reminds me of my own awakening. I could finally see my female self as Divine, acceptable, raw material to be used by Spirit. Before this, as a woman in the Catholic Church, I had no value or significance. I was a nobody simply because of my anatomy.

After mass, I stayed and sought out this remarkable woman who had provided this extraordinary experience. She was middle-aged, of medium height, and had a tinge of gray in her short, curly, brown hair. I asked her if she would be willing to talk to me about her experience with the priesthood. I followed up with a phone call, a visit, and new resources to explore. This was an exciting beginning of my transformation from a good Catholic girl to an advocate and activist for women.

Many years have passed since that remarkable encounter. Even as I wrote this story, I remember how profoundly every part of me responded to this experience. Even today, thirty years later, it touches who I am and what I do. It was a subtle but profound realization that embodied female spiritual leadership is possible. Today it's my hope that I personify and manifest the Divine Feminine in who I am and what I do. Truthfully, I had no idea it was possible until that day in January so long ago.

This event informs how I see the world, how I walk in the world, and the reason I'm writing this book. It informs how I see my role with my family, with money, and how I work to create a world I want for my grandkids and future generations. I have discovered that money is just one tool in our storehouse of resources to impact our world. But for me, the spiritual self is the inner powerhouse, and it cannot be measured. We can't quantify caring, compassion, community, communication, or love, but they are vitally important as well. We will utilize all these resources as we change our money paradigm, heal our money story, and take action using money as a tool to heal the world.

Affirmations

- I am grateful for the resources in my life.
- I am so pleased to be here, honoring my soul, my story, and my money.
- There is a divine plan for my life, my work, and my money.

Chapter 2
Preparation and Tools for the Journey

The best thing you can do for yourself is to invest in one thing that really matters—YOU.
—Anonymous

This book includes rituals, prayers, journaling, affirmations, and exercises to honor your money path. This is an opportunity to connect deeply with your spiritual self and the wider world of economics. This is a practice of walking in the world as a person with values, spirit, and inner self. Perhaps you might call it your soul journey.

Seasons

Each of us has lived through many seasons during our lives. We have lived through the seasons of infancy, childhood, adolescence, and adulthood, perhaps now moving toward old age. We have watched the tree grow from seed to seedling, from a small tree to a mature tree that produces flowers, fruit, and seeds. We know the transformation of the butterfly from an egg to a caterpillar, to a chrysalis, to a butterfly. Seasons are the frames of time, a lens to view the world. We deeply know that each season has its gifts and its challenges. We know there are changes with each season. Life does not remain static. Our inner selves, our financial situation, and the outside world are constantly changing, so please be gentle with yourself. Money can trigger us, challenge us, or overwhelm us. It can also jazz us, delight us, and foster security and confidence. It's a journey; let's see where we end up!

As we walk through the seasons of money, we start the journey with the season of Winter. It is our current and often cold relationship with money, finances, and our personal financial history. It's the world of finances in which we find ourselves operating, thinking, and managing our resources. It is where we find ourselves today so we can begin thinking about tomorrow. As we work with our money story, we can move into Spring and the planting of new seeds. In Spring, we will explore education and the role of financial literacy and take a look at what matters most in life. With our seeds planted, and our financial house in place, we move to the season of Summer. Summer is a time of growth, but also a time of tending to the weeds, the weather, and the wisdom of new choices. We move out into the world of options and decisions. We look at our role as consumers and our place in the world as local residents and as global citizens. Our journey together ends with harvest, in Autumn. We contemplate a sharing economy, the role of investing, and moving forward as we create choices and decisions for a just, kind, regenerative world.

Tools

As you prepare for this journey through the seasons, I recommend a few basic tools to take with you.

- Exercises—The exercises are meant to help you see money through a new lens, to heal your money story, or to identify ways to use money as a tool to create and transform your world. If an exercise seems particularly difficult for you, you can choose not to do it, but make sure to ask yourself if it is something you are avoiding or if it actually would not be helpful. Sometimes the most insight comes from doing the most difficult exercises.

- Affirmations—Affirmations are little prayers, thoughts, and reminders of how we want to think, and prompts about staying focused on our course. Please use them or create your own and place those motivations on your desk or in your calendar, frame a favorite affirmation, or do a litany of all of them as part of your morning meditation. Choose one that resonates deeply and say it daily for a week.
- Journal—Get a journal, preferably one you like, with a beautiful cover, and maybe some inspirational quotes inside (or add your own quotes). I have a money journal where I track my moods, inspiration, ideas, plans, and thoughts. It is not where my financial records are kept; it's a personal chronicle of my internal movement through my money world. You can use this journal for the exercises in this book.
- Weekly money date—This is a time to review your financial activities, and keep track of your income, expenses, and plans for your wise use of money, and to practice gratitude. I recommend you schedule your weekly money date on your calendar and be faithful to your commitment to this time.
- Meditation—Meditation is often referred to as mindfulness or as presence practice. Sit in a chair or on a cushion, cross-legged, or with your feet on the floor. Place your hands comfortably in your lap with spine straight. Allow the silent stillness to enter your body, your mind, and your heart. Observe your breath, in… out… in… out…. If thoughts arise, allow them to float down and out of your mind. If you become distracted by thoughts, focus again on your breath. Sit until you feel complete and ready to proceed with your day.

- Daily or weekly walk—I find that a daily walk keeps me moving, physically, mentally, and emotionally and helps with all things financial. It's a great way to have long conversations with yourself.

- Gratitude—Having a gratitude practice is a profoundly impactful way to remember and honor all the gifts, blessings, and beauty in life. Writing your gratitude list in your journal, doing a brief thank you at the beginning and end of each day, or taking time to appreciate each time you engage with money are great ways to incorporate gratitude into daily life.

- Altar—This may not be for everyone. But I find having a personal altar is a way to bring together spiritual symbols that have meaning. Using symbols, colors, or tokens of the season, or symbols of nature such as flowers, stones, or feathers, makes an altar a special way to connect with our divinity. Use symbols of abundance such as coins or dollars, special words, or intentions to focus your personal and financial work.

- Prayer—I define prayer as a way of connecting with the Divine, however you define the Divine in your life. "Nothing could matter less than what we call this force. I know some ironic believers who call God Howard, as in 'Our Father, who art in Heaven, Howard be thy name.'"[3] Personally, I like the words *Spirit, Divine, Universe, Goddess*, or *Beloved.* Others call this Wisdom, the Cosmos, or Grace—Howard works in a pinch—or just a deep breath is sometimes enough to remember and feel the sacredness within.

- Ritual—During our time together, we will celebrate several rituals. I define a *ritual* as a ceremony to honor and celebrate an intention. We will celebrate our money with sacred space and sacred time because that is what money is, a sacred tool. Rituals require intention, a bit of preparation, time, and a return to our connection to Source, however you define Sacred Source. The art, play, and practice of creating rituals may not be familiar to you, however, it can be learned. Some people have a natural talent for creating rituals, some have the training, and some people just do whatever feels right. I recommend you do what works for you. Rituals allow us to connect with our focus, connect with our Source, and feel our body. Ritual is a beautiful way to celebrate yourself and recognize there is no need for a middle woman or middleman. You are the priestess, priest, or holy one as you perform your ceremony. This is a non-hierarchical, expansive way to connect with the Divine. Ritual requires being present and being focused so we may connect with how we are, think, and use money and so we can be our best self.

This journey is about a new way to be, spend, and think about finances. We often don't have the words, the images, or the framework to pull money and spirit into the same picture. Ritual allows us to honor the wholeness of ourselves, our values, and our money. Rituals are directed *not* to the external outside world; they are directed to connect with the soul, your sacred inner self. There are elaborate rituals for calling in the directions, purification, consecrating space, healing journeys, and rites of passage. In this book, we will be using rituals for our intentions around money. There is also something special about sharing rituals with others. If it feels right, include others as you celebrate your ritual. For additional ritual resources, please see Appendix 1.

We often don't have the words, the images, or the framework to pull money and spirit into the same picture.

Beginning My New Money Journey Ritual

Preparation: Set the intention for your Beginning My New Money Journey ritual. Choose a time when you have thirty minutes to an hour. Clean a bit of space in your home or office or set up outside in nature. Choose a couple of beautiful items to bring to your setting, for example, a cloth, a stone, flowers, or a figurine that has meaning. Bring a candle and a match to light your candle. Arrange your items with love and intention to bring beauty to your setting. Bring some cash, a credit card, or a bank statement, and place them with your candle. This is an opportunity to bless your money and your journey. All rituals are based on intention. Remember to adapt it to fit your definition of Divine Source.

Begin: Light Your Candle. Sit in silence; pay attention to your inhale and exhale. Allow your body to relax and your mind to quiet. As thoughts arise, let them go.

Invocation:

> *Divine Source, God/Goddess, Giver of Life, Holy One,*
>
> *I call on You, Source Energy, I invite all my seen and unseen support, angels, and spirit guides to be with me now. I ask you to be with me as I walk this path to connect and unite my spirit and my money. I call my spirit, my heart, my soul to center on the Wholeness and the Holiness of being in the world, but not of the world. I release all that does not serve me. I am ready to heal my money story and realize a new money paradigm. I call in balance, harmony, grace, ease, and flow. I commit to*

tending my spiritual life as well as my financial life with compassion and tenderness as I work to create a just, sustainable world.

Ritual Body

Body and Money Blessing: Speak these words lovingly to yourself.

Bless my body that I may serve and honor You in all I do.

Bless my eyes that I may see clearly.

Bless my mouth that I may speak with honesty and truth.

Bless my ears that I may hear Your wisdom.

Bless my hands that I may work to create a just, sustainable world.

Bless my heart that I may be filled with love.

Bless my womb, or my seed, a place of creation that I may birth and nurture a grace-filled world.

Bless my legs that I may honor my own strength.

Bless my feet that I may walk always with You.

Bless this money and these symbols of money, that they may serve You.

Bless this money journey, bless my money, my resources, and my intentions to have a good relationship with money.

Bless me, Goddess, I am Yours.[4]

1. *Sit in silence and hear what your heart and your inner soul self have to say about this intention. If there is no inspiration, simply continue to breathe deeply and say thank you for this time.*

2. *Repeat your intention aloud. "Today I begin a new relationship with money. I commit to creating a world that works for me and the greater good." Feel your commitment and visualize what your world would look like and how you would feel. (Do you feel light, pleased, at peace, whole, or complete?) Feel that feeling, give it color, weight, and form. Feel it deeply and let that feeling settle in your heart and in the core of your body.*

3. *Sit in gratitude for this feeling. If you only find chaos and pain, go back to your breath and breathe in calm and white light. When you feel complete, close your ritual.*

Closing Blessing:

Beloved, I give thanks for this time, for these intentions, and for these insights. I open to the beauty around me (reach out your hands), I open to the beauty within me (hold your hands to your heart). So it is. Blessed Be.

Blow out your candle. Return to your day.

Affirmations

- Divine Wisdom guides and supports all my efforts with money.
- There is ease and flow as I work with my resources.
- I have all I need to create a full, rich, caring, compassionate life.

Part Two
Winter

Winter is a time of darkness, of silence, of rest, and a time when the land lies fallow. In the northern hemisphere, Winter Solstice is celebrated on December 21; in the southern hemisphere, it occurs on June 22. It is the shortest day and the longest night of the year. It's when the Earth is at its maximum tilt away from the Sun. It's also the day that the Sun begins its journey back to giving Earth a bit more light each day.

Winter can be a time of gifting, gratitude, and sharing. Those are wonderful qualities to cultivate. It's often a time of holiday sharing and gathering of family. However, in nature, winter is the season for going within, a season of quiet and mystery, of the darkness and the unknown. It is a retreat time. It is often a time to sit with what is; to deeply feel and know this present moment, in all the winter fog, fierceness, or frost. This time of the year can feel barren, chilly, and desolate, particularly when looking within. Winter is a period to allow silence and stillness. As with all things, patience and compassion are also to be your companions. This is an incubation stage to surrender what no longer serves you.

Winter is also a time to remember the role of cycles in our lives. In summer we revel in Nature's abundance, but in winter, when all seems frozen and gray, we can honor the stark, bare beauty of the leafless trees and the crystalline forms of frost on the window. The almost imperceptible increase in daylight is hardly noticeable, yet in our hearts and in the land, there is the hope and the anticipation of more light, more warmth with the coming change.

Is money wintery? A colleague once said to me, "Money is so cold and lifeless." As we focus on money, acknowledge your money story, the mystery, and the marvel that has brought you here today. Release what no longer serves you and set an intention to plant new seeds in your money garden. Now is a powerful time to die to the old to make room for the new. Winter is a wonderful time to ponder what you want to sow in your money and in life for the coming year.

In this season of winter, we begin our money journey with a Winter Ritual to honor where we are right now. Chapter 3 will be an examination of our societal money paradigm: what we as a society and culture believe, and how that needs to change. In Chapter 4, we move into reviewing and healing our personal money story. Chapter 5 is a special chapter for you as a woman or for the women in your life. Throughout Winter, we focus on reflecting.

Winter Ritual: Honoring Where You Are

Preparation: Gather and prepare items for a small fire. Alternately, you could prepare a candle and small fireproof vessel, such as a pan. Feel the energy of Winter, of the darkness, and of the cold. If it is not the season of winter where you live, find Winter solitude and retreat time. Make time to honor where you are in your life currently. Sit and acknowledge your current financial situation. Winter can be a fallow, barren time when things seem hidden. Sit in that mystery and take the opportunity to explore where you are and where you want to go on this journey of spirit and money. Make a list of your money challenges. On a separate page, list your feelings, experiences, and the opportunities you want to create.

Begin: Take a few deep centering breaths.

Opening Prayer:

> *Today I honor both the light and the dark. I honor this cycle of birth, life, death, and rebirth. I celebrate the return of the light, even as the land lies dormant, and the*

cold and dark are reminders of the season. I honor Gaia, Mother Earth, and God/Goddess in Her wisdom that Winter is part of the cycle of life. Holy Wholeness, I give thanks for this season of darkness and discernment.

Ritual: Take the list of your money challenges and acknowledge them one by one. When you feel ready or willing to release them, tear the paper into small pieces, and let them burn in the fire, thanking them for their role in your life. Allow those thoughts, stories, or patterns to be consumed by the flames. After you feel complete about your release of the old, hold your intentions for the new in front of you. Read this other list out loud to yourself five times, slowly, with strength and courage. Then hold it close to your heart and whisper it five times to your heart as you smile, allowing it to connect to your heart. Return your list to your money journal for safekeeping.

Closing Prayer: Beloved

Beloved, Keeper of my soul, I give thanks for this darkness.

Beloved Wisdom of the Winter, I breathe in your insights.

Beloved, Great Spirit of all, I release all that does not serve me.

Beloved Gate of Unknowing, I pass through this gate to be with You.

Beloved, Composer of the symphony of my life, I give thanks.

I lift to you my prayers and intentions, known and unknown, to ask for blessings of the highest and best outcome for this, my life.

Blessed Be, and So It Is.

End of Ritual

Affirmations

- I am grateful for the courage to begin this money journey.
- I have all the resources and Source support I need.
- I now create a just, sustainable world.

Chapter 3
Paradigm Shift from "Me, More, Mine" to "Us, We, and the Earth"

I don't want to protect the environment. I want to create a world where the environment doesn't need protection.
—Anonymous

Me, More, Mine, Greed, and Accumulation: Winter for Our Society

We live in the world of economics, finances, business, and work. It's the mechanism of employment and payment for services; it's the structure of businesses and organizations. It's the economic soup we have been swimming in for several hundreds of years. While many people have benefited from this economic order and under these circumstances, not everyone has profited from our current economic arrangement. This is the current collective Winter. It's time to reflect on the world around us.

Societally, there is a consumer philosophy that I define as the "Me, More, Mine" model. This model puts an emphasis on power, accumulation, greed, and scarcity. Up to now, this has been our money story and one that is in deep need of healing. Our recent global history is one of power, patriarchy, and colonialism. More telling, we have a history of domination, denigration, and disregard of women, the feminine, Nature, and Mother Earth. We have a sad past of pillaging the resources provided by the natural world. The old model of economics was focused on unlimited corporate and business growth and private wealth, with little consideration for the common good or for honoring and protecting Mother Earth. The tragic consequences of this thinking are evident in climate change, pollution, and the poisoning of our air, water, and land. Don't you think it's time for a shift in our thinking, our actions, and our financial systems? What about a new intention from Me, More, Mine to "Us, We, and the Earth"?

Societally, there is an expectation of continual and prolific production in our work and in our life. Look at the ads on TV or the magazine ads about how to grow your business, increase your income, or get healthier by doing more, going higher, better, faster. Our society values continual expansion and unlimited growth which is notably destructive to human life and nature. In the body, such growth is called *cancer*. This form of more, bigger, better, faster simply is not healthy. When we look at Mother Nature, we see how She has essential cycles and rhythms. These cycles are important; birth, growth, decay, and death are natural; continuous growth, with no rest or rejuvenation, and extraction without consideration for the consequences are the negative consequences of ignoring cycles and seasons.

While not everything that humans have created in the last few hundred years is wrong or bad, I propose that we evaluate our current relationship with money. Yes, we have had amazing improvements in health and education, and a reduction in poverty worldwide from a century ago. Technology has provided developments that include lifesaving medical advancements, the internet, and changing workplace technologies. In the context of human evolution, these advances have improved the world. However, these advances have not offered healing of the old story of *Me, More, Mine*, greed, and accumulation. Hence, it's time to move to a healthier vision of money and society, one that honors us as part of the Earth, not apart from Nature.

We are told by society advertising that we are weak, needy, inadequate, and have value only as consumers. Really, are you *only* a consumer? Of course not. You are a sacred being, in a deep relationship with others and the Earth. It's time to let go of this obsolete model of consumerism and think in terms of being a financial steward and a global citizen. We need to think about the impact of our money. What is the impact on people, employees, stakeholders, communities, and the environment? How can we as individuals apply our values to economic decisions that respect the Earth, stewardship, sufficiency, and "enoughness"? These are important questions.

As a consumer society, we have been trained to think that more is better. More money, a bigger house, a bigger paycheck—more, more, more is better. It's how business is designed: to be more, bigger, better, and faster than the competition. Additionally, we have been taught that monetary wealth equals self-worth. That is, if we have money, we have worth and value. Please remember, your value comes from being you. You have an appointment with life to be, live, and celebrate yourself. You are a manifestation of the Divine in bodily form, regardless of the dollars in your bank account.

One of my observations regarding books, programs, and courses about money is they focus on making more, having more, and getting more. Super-size everything, please! Think about it—it is simply not sustainable! Where is our new money story? Where is the language that honors us as human citizens of the Earth, as a global community? Where is the focus on the common good? Where is the language about using money to create a regenerative economy? Where is the language that supports our decisions to consider Mother Earth as Creatrix, provider, and sustainer? Have we considered that our job as inhabitants of the Earth is to nurture, support, and protect the Earth's resources, not just consume them?

Money is a tool that we can wield as a manifestation of the Divine. We are Spirit, and included in the world of Spirit is our money. Money, economics, or our societal structures are not separate from Spirit.

For example, let's look at knives, machetes, or big, heavy equipment. If there is a problem with using a dangerous tool, the issue comes from the person or administrator who is holding the tool and how the tool is being used. It's also about the policies that surround tools. It is the same with money. Money is not good or evil; it is how money is used. This is not about money versus spirit; this is about honoring that money is part of our spiritual life. The old system of *Me, More, Mine* may have worked for you, your family, or your community. However, that way of doing business has harmed and injured other people and communities around the world. Yes, we can do it differently.

We are moving as a society from *Me, More, Mine* to *Us, We, and the Earth.* It will take each of us to do our part, design our society, and be in communion with those who are not yet born.

But now is the time to take the opportunity to create a world that considers all of *Us*, the collective *We*, and our beautiful *Mother Earth.* Can we all be brave enough to work for the change we want to see in the world?

Me, More, Mine* or *Us, We, and the Earth

	OLD MODEL	NEW MODEL
World View	Me, More, Mine	Us, We, The Earth
Balance	Masculine	Masculine/Feminine
Divinity Recognized	Male God Only	Divinity Recognized
Resources	Extractive, Wasteful	Regenerative, Sustainable
Relationships	Patriarchal, Power Over	Cooperative, Collaborative
Work	Exploitive, Onerous	Just, Socially and Personally Enhancing
Self	A Cog in the Machine	Whole and Complete

Us, We, and the Earth

I invite you to consider a new story of money, finance, and economics. Let's think about *Us* and *We*, the collective We. This is a gentle, kinder approach for us and our world, and it includes honoring Mother Earth. This is a way that recognizes our interconnectedness and interdependence. It's about deliberate thinking and giving ourselves permission to think about the future we want for ourselves and our children, our grandchildren, and their children's children. It is a patient, gentle, life-affirming, regenerative way of being. It allows the market and the temple to link together for the benefit of the common good and for taking care of the Earth. It allows us to release the societal norms that keep us tied to the dollar, to profit, and to more, bigger, and better.

In Winter, we review our life and plan our new growth. We are bringing into focus a vision that looks further than the next paycheck, the next quarter's earnings, or the next investment. We can protect the common goods such as water, air, land, and infrastructure. This is our opportunity to support and fund the United Nations Sustainable Development Goals, a set of global goals, signed by 197 nations, to improve life on the Earth with the focus on people, planet, prosperity, peace, and partnership. We can advocate for local economies, celebrate our diversity, and consign legal rights and protection to Nature. This is our opportunity to create a world where real wealth is measured in love, connection, community, cooperation, and care, for others and our Earth. Each of us can do our small part by using our inner compass and our financial resources.

This is transformational thinking: an important change from the way things are to a new future and a different outcome. Here we are doing a revitalization, a shift in how we view, use, and invest money. It's alchemy: the transformation of money matter into a powerful tool of renewal.

Further, we live in an abundant, unlimited universe, internally and in our physical world as well. There is potential for us to light each other up by sharing our success, our money, our resources, our knowledge, and our gifts. In the old story, we were told that there are finite resources, limited money, finite job opportunities, and a shortage of resources. It is old thinking; for example, "If I have some (i.e., money, property, work) then others don't have (money, property, or work)." It's a scarcity mindset that keeps us held in the *Me, More, Mine* concept.

Moreover, when I do better, others do better, and when you thrive, I thrive. This is not a zero-sum game—this is lifting everyone so that we have enough for everyone's needs. We can focus our money, expertise, and action on designing a world of systems that work for everyone, that allow joy and fulfillment in our work and in our communities, and that engage our money for positive social and financial outcomes.

There are many people doing important work in the world to create a better world: people working on climate issues, sustainable agriculture, and social justice for all. There are Herculean efforts to clean up our oceans, eliminate poverty, save the environment, protect wildlife, and provide clean water and clean energy to communities. And all these efforts require caring, money, investment, and systems to ensure equitable access, community involvement, just allocation of resources, and respect for the environment.

In society, money and our sacred self are often disconnected. It's that split between the sacred and the profane, as defined by society. But what if it's all sacred? What if we come to see money as one more modality to engage in a sacred way with the world? Honoring and recognizing our Divine Connection to Goddess and God can move us to a place of integrating the feminine and the masculine, the yin and the yang, and connecting our spiritual self with our economic self. By integrating the Divine into our economic system, we can embody our inner goodness, our Divine nature, and our soul self into money, financial systems, and a new social order.

But what if it's all sacred? What if we come to see money as one more modality to engage in a sacred way with the world?

Perhaps now is the opportunity for us as a human race to redefine what we want our economic system to look like. We have been socialized to believe the best model is the one of profit, the one that focuses on consumption, greed, accumulation, short-term gains, and instant gratification. We have been educated, socialized, and tutored to want more, to accumulate more, and to buy more. It's the American way, right? The mall has become the center of the

> The tallest building in the town used to be the church. Now it's the bank. Is this where we want our focus?

community, where people gather, hang out, and everything is focused on buying the next new thing. The tallest building in the town used to be the church. Now it's the bank. Is this where we want our focus?

I want us to rethink profit, accumulation, and consumerism. Scholar and feminist theologian Sallie McFague, in her book *Blessed Are the Consumers: Climate Change and the Practice of Restraint,* calls consumerism "the most successful religion on the planet" with disastrous consequences for humanity and the Earth.[5] It's time to recognize the power of treating our money, our possessions, and the Earth with respect, honor, and care. How differently would our checkbooks, our wardrobes, our homes, our transportation, and our investments look if we chose to care for and employ them to benefit the world, not just ourselves?

You are a sacred being. You were born with unique gifts and talents. Your life path and mine is to discover, cultivate, and share those gifts. Some would call it talent or genius; others, dharma or divine destiny. As we cultivate a positive money story and make new money decisions, we also explore our own spiritual and personal growth. In doing so, each of us contributes our talents and gifts back into the world, sharing our very own version of greatness.

This may go against everything you believe about money, investing, finance, and the economy. This idea that we use money not just for ourselves but for the greater good and Nature may seem foreign to what you have been taught. It certainly is not the message society gives us about money and wealth. Perhaps this is something you have thought about but haven't investigated for yourself. Wherever you are on this journey, you are in the right place.

It is time for the conscious use of money, an economic revolution, and a reconfiguration in thinking, spending, saving, gifting, and investing. Let's take ownership and leadership of our own personal journey with money. Let's be conscious about money; we cannot leave it to outside forces, old stories, or what media or social constructs say. This is the time to do things from an inside perspective, inside you, your best self, your spiritual self, and your deepest values.

We know in our hearts that we give meaning to things, goods, and possessions. They may be more or less expensive or an item of sentimental value, but we decide what we value. I've been in big, beautiful homes that I had no interest in owning; I've been in small, simply furnished apartments that were a delight to experience. I have eaten at elegant restaurants and the local hole in the wall with equal gusto. There is much more to our lives than what we own, how much money we have, or the size of our investment fund. Yes, we need enough to be comfortable, but who I am is so much more important than what I have, accumulate, or own. The relationships we share, experiences of love, magical life moments, and our connection with nature are far richer than stuff.

We are meant to engage and encourage the inner essence of self. This is a time to connect with who you are with your checkbook, the life you live in your community, your activities, your investments, and your estate planning. You are a global citizen, working to improve our collective future. No, we cannot change everything by our own individual actions, but we can shift the paradigm from me to us, from mine to ours, and from consumer to Earth citizen.

Finally, let's recognize our deep interconnectedness with the Earth, our neighbors, locally and globally, and our dependence on a healthy ecosystem. Yes, this web of connections is vital. This book is about shaping a world where there is enough food, clean water, adequate infrastructure, education, and just wages. We can build a world community of respect for the Earth and all the gifts that Mother Earth so generously supplies. We can begin to see the beauty of the trees, mountains, and oceans as our relations and not just as resources to be mined for our benefit. It's time to respect and protect this precious relationship. We must honor the fact that we belong to the Earth, She does not belong to us. Nature is not where we go, but Mother Earth is where we live.

Our Challenging Winter Situation

There is so much uncertainty in the world. We know the world is in crisis. The headlines scream the stories daily: monetary crisis, the gap between the poorest and the wealthiest continues to grow, climate crisis, pandemics, sexism, racism, terrorism, housing crisis, the digital divide, earthquakes, hurricanes. The list goes on. Facing the future feels like a daunting challenge. Just as a reminder, there are also kind, compassionate people, like you, who want to change the way we currently live. Thank you for your caring and your willingness to use money as a tool to reshape our financial system and build a new healthier, regenerative economy.

The United States was built on capitalism power and privilege. The old paradigms of social, cultural, and political structures were born from patriarchy and colonization. The current United States economy is built on a historical foundation of privilege, power, and domination by the white male culture. It is a harsh and uncompromising system. Exploitation, slavery, and oppression were seen as a victory for the conquerors; the stories of the vanquished often disappeared. The big themes of power, greed, accumulation, and disregard for the Earth, Earth's resources, and other species are a sad part of our human history.

Racism and sexism are part of the systemic oppression that has been a mainstay of our economic system. We can acknowledge that people of color and women now have rights that were not available in the past. We have Black people running for office, women running large businesses, Indigenous leaders appointed to national offices, and a recognition that inclusion and diversity are vitally important to a healthy society.

At the core of much of our economic and financial frameworks is the idea that we are separate. *We are not separate!* We are all on this Earthship as global citizens. We are connected by nature, by relationships, by technology, and by economics. I like to think of it as the Stone Soup story, where if we all added our bit of harvest from the garden, then eventually, we could all share in the soup. But if she won't share her potato, and he won't bring his carrots, and I refuse to add my onion, and you are unwilling to share your turnip, then none of us are able to partake in the feast of sharing, of food, or of relationships.

We cannot maintain our current economic system with this myopic and short-sighted emphasis on accumulation and greed. We have already seen the devastation of the old model of capitalism, patriarchy, and disregard and disrespect for Mother Earth. Our consumer society has flooded us with messages that life, money, and society are all about Me, all about More, all about Mine.

Perhaps it's time to take a deep breath and decide what we personally want for ourselves and for our world, rather than letting the external world decide for us. Do you remember the bumper sticker "He who dies with the most toys, wins"? What if we begin to see that "She who shares the most money and love, wins!" What a radical concept!

Yes, it all seems like too much—too much poverty, sadness, war, and inequality. Yes, I want the world to be better, but my minuscule effort seems so pitiful, so meaningless, so inconsequential. I know that thinking. I face it every day. So do our neighbors across the street, the second-grade teacher, the barista at the coffee shop, and the Wall Street financier. But if we can remember that each of us has an impact, we each can do something, even if it seems so inconsequential. Every decision and each dollar have an impact. If we can remember it's the little things that make the big difference, then the question is, what impact do you want to have? What impact do you want your dollar to have? What is the world that you want to create with your spirit and your dollars?

For too long, society has seen patriarchy and male-dominated power commanding the economic and political engines of our society. But denying others because of race, sex, economic status, or global location means that we have a world administered by a fraction of the human potential, governed by a fraction of the human experience, and guided by a fraction of the human heart. The consequences if we don't change this paradigm are dire. So, let's change the paradigm and do our part.

EXERCISE

Your Vision for a World That Works for All

In your money journal, write your vision for a world that works for all, humans and non-humans, and Mother Earth. What is your vision for a world that works for now and for the next seven generations? Envision a world that has enough: enough resources, enough food and water. Write about a world that has enough infrastructure, enough education, enough jobs, and enough money circulating. Write about a world where there is enough knowledge, kindness, compassion, and willingness to correct injustice, inequity, and oppression. What would that world look like to you? When you finish, select a few key points. Write those points out and post them on a whiteboard or type it out and post it on your bulletin board or frame it and hang it on the wall. For example, right now my whiteboard has the thought: "Imagine a world if the majority of the money was in conscious caring hands: I see a life-preserving, restorative, regenerative world!" It's part of my daily inspiration.

Affirmations

- ❖ I am a powerful cocreator and perfectly suited to do this work.
- ❖ I believe and work for a just, sustainable, kind, and regenerative world.
- ❖ I choose to respond calmly and gracefully to my finances and money situation.

Chapter 4
Money Story

My story is a freedom song of struggle. It is about finding one's purpose, how to overcome fear and to stand up for causes bigger than one's self.
—Coretta Scott King

My Winter Money Story

As we do our Winter reflections, I offer my own story to spark yours.

As a child, my Grandpa Felipe would write letters and tape a quarter to the bottom of the letter. My Grandma Virginia would send me a dollar each year for my birthday. Having money was not part of my childhood. My basic needs were met, and money didn't factor into my life in a big way. I didn't have money, and I didn't spend money.

I was born into a Roman Catholic, Mexican American family of five children, the oldest child, and the only girl. My father was a mechanical engineer, and my mother was a stay-at-home mom. I grew up in the 1960s in a modest tract home in the growing city of Albuquerque, New Mexico with my mother, my father, and four younger brothers. My parents both grew up speaking Spanish and were punished at school as a result. Consequently, I didn't learn

Spanish. But what I did learn was the Mexican American ways of how to be female in a male-dominated culture.

We often had frijoles (pinto beans), chile, and freshly made tortillas. During Lent, torta de huevo (egg omelets) was on the menu and a family favorite was caldito (hamburger and potato stew). In the spring, the winds blew off the Sandia Mountains, my mother cut lilacs, and we hunted Easter eggs in the backyard. In the summer, we harvested fresh tomatoes from the big garden in the backyard, played in the open mesa behind our house, and ran in the sprinklers. In the fall, we raked the oak leaves in the front yard, put up fruits and vegetables from the local farmers, and got very excited about new school supplies. In the winter, we built a fire in the fireplace, made tamales, and baked dozens of cookies for Christmas. Those are the good memories.

I also grew up knowing my role and place in the family. The women in the family were wives, mothers, daughters, sisters, aunties, housewives, housekeepers, and, while considered necessary, not really individuals themselves. They were roles: a cook, a housekeeper, a driver, a caregiver, or a support person. But a woman was not really an individual who had dreams, desires, goals, or aspirations of her own. Her role was to support her man and the men in the family. The men made the money, and the women stayed home and took care of the family.

Both of my parents came from families with eight children. Apart from one uncle, everyone was married, everyone had children, and that was our social life: family. Women had the role of providing food, taking care of kids, keeping them out of the way of the men, and cleaning up. Kids could play, unless of course, you were an adolescent female, then your role was to take care of the little kids. The men did "manly" things like playing music, singing, target shooting, playing poker, and drinking. The roles were very defined, and the tasks associated with the roles were clear.

What I remember learning about money is that Dad made the money, Mom spent what was necessary, and only what was absolutely necessary, nothing more, nothing extra. My mother taught me to be frugal—extremely frugal. She made most of our clothes, she cooked at home, and we did not go out to eat. My dad was very handy with tools and mechanics, so we had skateboards made from planks of wood and old skates. My dad loved bargains and would bring home projects, rebuilding a bike, an engine, or a piece of furniture. Buying something new was always a novelty, like getting new clothes for school. It was a big deal at our house.

In our home, Dad took care of the money. When he sat down at the kitchen table with the checkbook to pay bills, everyone, including my mother, gave him a wide berth. This is where he commanded the house. He paid the bills, he took care of the money, and he bought lots of insurance, telling us he wanted to take care of us. He was the one responsible for the money. My mother, me, and my brothers all stayed out of the way.

I have very little memory of having my own money. As I grew older, I did receive an allowance, but I don't remember how much, or ever having much of my own money. I was taken care of by my family, so having money of my own was not necessary. As I grew, I worked as a babysitter, a clerk at TG&Y Five & Dime, and did food prep at Tijuana Taco in high school. Yes, I was paid, and I promptly spent it. I wasn't a saver. No one taught me about money, how to reconcile a checkbook, or how the stock market worked. It was not a consideration, because I was so clueless and uninformed; I was also indifferent to money. If I had the money, I spent it; if I didn't, oh well… I worked or made do with what I had. It was also a carefree attitude about money. I liked it when I had money, but I didn't fret or worry about it when I didn't have it. I had no idea how ignorant or oblivious I was about finances.

I do remember a conversation with my dad when I was getting ready to go to college. He told me he would pay for each of us to go to college. The caveat was that when my brothers finished college, they would have to pay him back half of what he paid in college expenses. For me, however, I wouldn't have to pay him back because he didn't want to burden my husband with my debt. The norms, expectations, and decisions were different if you were female. In reality there were some savings bonds and with that assistance, I worked and paid my own way through undergraduate school. To pay for my master's degree, I took out school loans. Graduate school was the beginning of a realization that I needed to work and create income to pay back my school loans. But I wanted to work. I wanted to participate in the labor force. I was educating myself to participate in a professional position and hopefully contribute to society.

After I married and had children, I was committed to raising my children and not working full time. I didn't want my kids in daycare all day, and I had four young boys; daycare was expensive. However, there was another part of me that longed to work professionally, to use my skills and talents. I struggled with bouts of depression and a sense of being a failure. While parenting four small people every day, there's not much feedback on how well you are doing. In my mind, I mostly saw the mess, the chaos, the undone chores, and the many things I wanted to do that didn't get done because I was a young, overwhelmed, stay-at-home mother.

Money was such a hard topic in our house. My husband made the money, and I tried to spend as little as possible. When I did want to purchase something, it always felt like a battle. It wasn't a battle for things he wanted, like new couches when we did our home remodel or flooring for his office. He wanted high quality and something that would last a long time. But beautiful things, such as new dishes, and the words foo-foo, elegant, and spontaneous are not in his makeup.

I tried, I really tried. I bought most of the clothes for me and the boys at thrift stores, which I actually liked and still like to do. I don't like paying $60.00 or $80.00 for a blouse that I can get for $6.00 or $8.00 at the thrift store. I was very frugal when I was a young mother. I read books on saving money; I made lists of the stores where I could get bulk items, and I clipped coupons and shopped with advertisements. When I was pregnant with my third son, I found a book at the library called *Once-A-Month Cooking* by Mary Beth Lagerborg and Mimi Wilson. I taught myself how to plan thirty meals. I would shop for all the ingredients one day and then find a babysitter for the next day and spend it cooking all day. I would have meals in the freezer for a month. I would make two to three gallons of pasta sauce, four chicken broccoli casseroles, three meatloaves, a gallon of bean and corn soup, and package it all up and have meals where I added a vegetable and a salad and I could feed my family of six economically, without spending all day, every day, in the kitchen.

I homeschooled my kids when they were young. Paul ate breakfast at work but with four boys at home all day, I was preparing three meals a day for six of us for about seven years until they began attending school during mid-high. I kept track of how much I spent on food and other items for our household, but it didn't include much for play or luxury. We rarely went out to eat as a family. Paul and I had a weekly lunch; we would go out to eat each week at one of the small restaurants near his office. I would hire a babysitter for that hour, and that was the forty-five minutes that we had each week to talk things over.

When it came to money, Paul did it all. He paid the bills, reconciled the checkbook, and handled the banking, the credit cards, the car, the house, and health insurance. He made the investments. He tried to get me to participate; he invited me to meetings with our financial advisers. He would talk me into taking care of the bills, and I would pay them, but then, I would make mistakes, I would be late, and I wouldn't get something paid. It was a struggle for me. He would get frustrated and then just do it himself. It seemed easier for both of us. But there was always tension. My primary feeling about money was that "I can never do it right." There was always this sadness and guilt that I was spending too much, not doing it right, and that my decisions were wrong. It was a challenge. I never felt good about money or the way I was handling it. We did things simply, which is fine. But in spite of spending the smallest amount possible, we still had four kids that needed things as they grew. We limited birthday parties for the boys. We had a party when they turned six and ten; otherwise, on their birthday, they could invite one friend over for a birthday dinner. We limited their activities to one activity at a time. Ostensibly the reason was I didn't want to be driving all the time to take them to various activities, but I think it was a matter of money. Each of the activities—Scouts, bowling, soccer, and bike racing—cost both time and money. We bought used furniture and used appliances (except when our refrigerator stopped working), we went camping, we didn't go out to eat, we didn't go to movies, and instead of big vacations, we visited family. Luxury and extravagance were not part of our doings or our budget. We spent only what was necessary, the rest was put in savings.

The issue to me was that I didn't feel like those savings were available to me. I didn't know how much was there, I didn't have access to it, and I felt like it was this big pit, where all our money went, except for what was absolutely necessary for living, nothing extra. We had a budget, yes, and there was a category called Flit, which was fun money, but that was for renting a movie or going for ice cream. It didn't include buying new dishes or a trip to the ocean.

I love beautiful things. I love luxury, beautiful clothes, magnificent art, fresh flowers, beautiful dishes, and antiques. I love art, music, theater, dance, and travel. I love staying in hotels, eating out, strolling in downtown shops, and perhaps buying a trinket. I love beautiful jewelry. I own many beautiful pieces of jewelry because Paul knows I love jewelry, and for some reason, it's okay to buy me jewelry. But the rest—travel, luxury, extravagance, and spontaneous spending—are not part of the way we live.

I remember one summer when the kids were in high school. Each year Paul would go on a backpacking trip. He was gone for the week, and the boys were busy. I had been wanting a new bike. I had an old, used bike that belonged to my dad. Paul had put a new chain on it and the tires were okay, but the gears never worked well, and it was an old, beat-up bike that was well-used. Like many things in my life, it was adequate, if one didn't care about looks, comfort, or functionality.

After thinking about it for several days, I went to our local bike shop to look around and see what was available. It was an emotional and intense visit to the bike shop. I wanted a new bike, but spending money on myself, for something that I wanted, just because I wanted it, well, that wasn't how our money program worked. As much as I wanted a new bike, I couldn't justify the expense. I knew we had the money. But would I be willing to spend it on a new bike for me?

I found a bike I liked, a brand-new, black, Trek mountain bike, comfortable, with gears that worked! It was a gem of a bike! I took it out for a ride around the neighborhood. I took it back, wanting it, but not knowing how to buy something new and expensive for myself. I went for a long walk and talked myself in and out of buying a new bike. It was an old money story that somehow, it wasn't worth buying something new for myself. I remember crying like I wanted to deserve this bike, but somehow, I didn't deserve it. I spent what seemed like hours doing Emotional Freedom Technique, EFT (see the explanation in Appendix 1: Tools for Healing Your Money Story), and I went for several long walks. I wanted a new bike, but I didn't feel free to buy it or to allow myself to treat myself to a new bike. It was a long, painful week. In the end, I bought myself the bike, but even now, many years later, I remember how intense and agonizing it was to decide to buy myself the bike. I realize now I had unhealthy beliefs around spending money on myself.

This money thing has been painful for a long time. I have felt so inadequate, incompetent, and incapable of making and managing money. It seemed like the only thing I knew how to do was to spend as little as possible.

I started my healing money journey in a serious way in January 2013. I wrote in my money journal that I was ready to move from being a "money dummy" to being a "conscious investor." I started in the blustery, cold, dark part of Winter, deciding to seek a way to grow myself and my money relationship as I traveled through learning about money. Part of my money story was steeped in fear, my fear of not doing it right. This is something I have really struggled with over the years. I fear I will make bad decisions, and that my husband, my family, or others will dismiss, ridicule, or scorn my efforts to work with money. I know what it's like to not understand financial statements and to be confused about funds or financial structures like IRAs (Individual Retirement Accounts). I am familiar with the overwhelm by too many notes, files, statements, or details. I want approval for my efforts and often feel like a failure trying to understand what is out there in the financial world. I know how it feels to feel inferior, inadequate, and hopeless, like I will never be able to comprehend all the aspects of money and investing. I know the feeling of a queasy stomach, of tears welling up in my eyes, of the tightness in my throat when I'm trying hard to share my thoughts or concerns.

To begin, I bought a spiral notebook, put a big *$* sign on the front with a marker, and started writing down my goals, notes about things I was reading, and videos I watched. In February of that year, I wrote my goal: "to get information for me to be responsible and literate about money." I'm still on that journey. I was also inspired by Arthur Ashe's quote, "Start where you are and do what you can."

Initially, all I could see were the challenges. I was spending too much. I wasn't working at the time; I had health challenges, and I felt disappointed in myself because I wasn't contributing money to our family. I felt challenged because I was married to a marvelous man, a practicing CPA, who appeared to me to have all our money knowledge, organization, and access. He knew all the rules and understood all the sensitive and confidential information about our money. I had allowed that to happen, but the real fact was, that I didn't know much about our money situation. Yes, I was familiar with our bills and my credit card expenses, and we talked about a budget, but I wasn't exactly sure how I fit into the decision-making on how we used our money. Regarding our investments, savings, or retirement money, I really was quite clueless. I felt inadequate and ill-prepared to discuss these issues with such a knowledgeable person, even if he was my husband.

I recognized that I did not have the financial knowledge or literacy to be a full partner in our financial discussions. It was time for me to step up and learn about money and money management. With that insight, I began my financial education. I bought financial literacy books and courses, watched YouTube videos, journaled, and used EFT to work on my issues about money. In the process, I realized I had never been taught about money. My parents didn't teach me about money. My dad paid the bills, and my mother was frugal, to the point of being austere, so I thought that's what it meant to be a woman, to be frugal. Another issue that came up for me at that time is that I have four brothers. They are all successful professionals. I was a stay-at-home mother for many years. I was comparing my professional and financial success to my siblings. I did not feel successful either professionally or financially. It was time to change that. I wanted to be an active participant in our financial choices. So, I began my new relationship with finances, money, and myself.

I am still finding my own voice, my own thinking, and my own power to spend, use, and invest money in ways that will benefit the bigger world, not just my small world. I am standing in my personal power to be a good steward of my resources. I am sharing what I have learned with you.

Your Money Beliefs and Story

It has been my privilege through my work, conferences, and community to hear many money stories. All of the stories are true. Some of the names and details have been changed for privacy.

When my client Leah looked at her money story, it was all about the pain of growing up with little money and a father who saw everyone who had money as greedy and a bad person. When she wrote her money story, it was one of pain, grief, and sorrow about money, not having enough, wanting more, and being taught to believe that having money made you a selfish, unkind, awful human being. Unraveling that story, she did not want to be a person who was an awful human, and she wanted to change her money story, to allow money to be a source of joy and comfort instead of pain and anguish. After working with her money story, seeing it as a river where she was always supported, she was able to release her old story and begin a new relationship with her money.

Ivanna grew up in Ukraine in a family that was quite poor, and her family remembered the history of starvation in her small community when communism came and took the foodstuffs, leaving nothing for the village. During that time, it was dishonorable for anyone to have money because only the elite was allowed to have it. Now, as she is transitioning into having a job, and being responsible for her family, the old story that having money is dishonorable no longer works for her. Healing her money story has allowed her to increase her income, her savings, and interestingly, someone who owed her money in the past, recently and unexpectedly repaid a long overdue loan.

We all have our beliefs about money. They come from our parents, our family, our culture, and our upbringing. You have probably heard the following:

- Money is the root of all evil.
- What, do you think money grows on trees?
- Rich people are bad.
- Money is for spending.
- It's selfish to want money.
- It's more virtuous to be poor.
- Women can't take care of money.
- There's not enough.
- It's selfish to spend money on yourself.
- Money is hard to come by.

Each of us has a money story that influences our decisions about earning, spending, saving, and how we interact with the world. What is your internal dialogue about money? Slow down, breathe, and recognize this is part of your story. In her book, *Radical Acceptance: Embracing Your Life with the Heart of a Buddha,* Tara Brach notes, "Through the sacred art of pausing, we develop the capacity to stop hiding, to stop running away from our experience. We begin to trust in our natural intelligence, in our naturally wise heart, in our capacity to open to whatever arises."[6]

Each of us has a money story that influences our decisions about earning, spending, saving, and how we interact with the world. What is your internal dialogue about money?

Spend time with me as we wander through this sacred land called you. Let's see if we can figure out how to be in a grateful, kind relationship with money. We can figure this out. I've been there: fearful, feeling powerless, and not knowing how to take the next right step. Just take the first step. That is the wonderful thing about life, we just need to do the next thing, and we don't have to figure it all out before we start. Breathe into the next step; let's do this together.

Money and our history with money shape us and how we respond to our world. Thinking about our money story allows us to reflect on our experiences and assumptions about money. Equally important, as we move through this process, this is not about blame or shame. We are not broken or in need of repair. We come into this world whole, and complete, and now is the time to come into a full relationship with your money self. We begin by uncovering our thoughts, beliefs, and historical relationship with money.

Maybe you grew up wealthy and were ashamed of having so many things. You may have had to drop out of school to work and support your family. Perhaps you relied on your partner for support and missed out on career opportunities. Or perhaps you have worked full-time since you were sixteen years old, and the thought of not working makes you feel like you have no value if you are not earning money. Each of these scenarios impacts how you interact with money now.

Money has a certain flavor in our lives. Often stressful, fearful, or challenging, these feelings can cause us to feel small, unworthy, or incompetent. "I'll never understand this." "I'm too far behind to ever get caught up." "I don't have value if I don't bring in an income." It can also make us feel exhilarated, delighted, or celebratory! "I balanced my checkbook!" "I finished my taxes!" "I saved $500!" "I paid off my credit card!"

We use money every day: earning, spending, saving, and investing. Often, we don't even think about how we are using our money. This book is your chance to become thoughtful and conscious about your financial decisions. Instead of living by default, we can live by design.

So, let's design the kind of relationship we would like to have with money. Take charge, internally, as the responsible person, the decision maker, the director, and the producer in the movie of your life.

In many ways, it doesn't matter if you have a lot of money or very little. If we are not tending to it, developing a relationship with it, and caring for the details of maintenance and management, then you will be uncomfortable. My friend Guadalupe raised two children by herself on the outskirts of town in an old trailer, working as a house cleaner. But she was careful, thoughtfully stretched every penny, and saved. We helped her buy her first house because I knew how careful she was with money and that she would be able to pay us back.

Often, we spend money because it makes us feel good, satisfied, or content, even if only for a few moments. We like instant gratification, we like the thing, the item, the new, and the fulfillment of having, owning, or possessing this purchase. We like the feeling that having, or spending, gives us. It's a bit like eating: It's immediate satisfaction. Unfortunately, tending to money is generally not quick or as delightful as spending on the next shiny object, good coffee, or our online wish list. However, there are steps, processes, thinking, and intentions that go into building a relationship with your finances.

We often want more money, thinking it will make things better. But what we want is what money can give us. We want what money can do, not really the money itself. Having lots of money does not ensure your life will be perfect, wonderful, or happy. Many people with money are unhappy or feel burdened and oppressed by the responsibility of money. Money provides us with security, safety, and ways to take care of ourselves and our families. Money can allow freedom for creating joy, art, relationships, and fun. Money can be a source of hope, inspiration, and creativity. It can give rise to dreams, a trip to Europe, a master's degree, a new carpet, or funds to pay off debt. It can be a source of generosity by caring for others.

Money is also an uncomfortable, emotionally charged topic in our society. My friend Alex says "We all have our sh*t about money; it's not the same sh*t, but we all have it." We worry about it, we want more, or we wish someone else would take care of it for us. We fear running out of money. We dread looking at our bank accounts, paying bills, or we fret about our mounting credit card debt. It can be a source of anxiety, conflict, major disagreements, emotional hurt, and sadness. It can also be a source of comfort, blessing, support, or selflessness.

With all the other challenging aspects of our life including work, family, home, health, and daily news crises, adding money to our list of concerns can be overwhelming. Learning and personal growth can be uncomfortable. No, you may not be an expert on all these financial topics. But you wouldn't be reading this book if you weren't ready to step out of your comfort zone and move into a new and different relationship with money. Yes, it requires a choice, it requires commitment, and it means doing things differently. It is also an opportunity to look at this through the lens of compassion and kindness. It's connecting your money self and your soul self.

Maybe part of your new self-talk is about allowing yourself permission to explore, investigate, travel into this new alliance, to create a new bond with your sacred self and how you engage with money. Alternatively, what will happen if you don't change? What is the price of staying in your old ways of thinking, doing, and being? What is the cost of not moving forward? How do you really want to feel about yourself and your money?

I want to acknowledge that this can be a rough and rocky road. Yes, it can be overwhelming. Yes, it can be deep emotional work. Yes, you must uncover and begin a new relationship with money. Yes, you must think about the world you want to create for the future, but, even so, shouldn't we be doing that anyway? Money can be a catalyst for transformation, a revolution, or an evolution to accelerate and create the life you love.

> Money can be a catalyst for transformation, a revolution, or an evolution to accelerate and create the life you love.

Another way is to change finance by financing change. You can find places that do good work, that create the change you want to see in the world, and that target your money to support those efforts.

A New Money Story

We change because we make a decision to change. We can't lose twenty-five pounds in a week; we can't get out of fifteen thousand dollars of credit card debt in a month. Perhaps you think you can't change because you are too old, too ill, too busy, too broke, too in debt, or a variety of excuses that limit your perception of possibility and keep you from getting what you want. Changing our money story takes patience, awareness, compassion, and time. My big shift was when I realized that I really did want to move from a "money dummy to a conscious investor." That was my goal. It didn't happen overnight, but I do feel like I now make decisions that support my goal. In many ways, this new story is about having a new relationship with your money. It's about spending time getting to know yourself and your money. Begin like it's a first date, get to know yourself and your money a bit at a time, setting time aside to say hello. After a few dates, you can start putting plans in place.

This is about a shift in mindset, reversing the personal or societal programming that you have lived with your entire life. It's about setting the stage for personal responsibility and financial well-being. It's about learning to be creative in how you present yourself to the world, spiritually and financially. This next exercise will help you design a new money story for yourself.

EXERCISE

Your Money Story, Old and New

This is a two-part exercise to be done over a couple of days.

Part I: My Old Money Story

Set a time to reflect on your money journey. Have your journal with you.

Allow your mind to rest and allow memories to come to you. As you read through this list, respond to these questions. Choose one or two that resonate with you.

- What's your earliest memory of money?
- What beliefs, attitudes, or family experiences affected your relationship with money?
- As you grew to be a young adult, what was your experience with earning, spending, and saving?
- As an adult, what experiences have impacted your decisions and attitudes about money?
- How has your relationship with money changed over time? How do you feel about money now?

There's no judgment here; this is a time to accept your story, honor your history, and be compassionate with yourself. As you journal these questions, reflect on the impact of your story. Honor and thank yourself and your story. Wait a day or so before working on your new money story.

Part II: My New Money Story

For this exercise, arrange for some time alone, to meditate, breathe, and set your intention to invite a new money story into your life. What would your new money story include? How would you look, feel, and act in your new money story? How would it change your life? Embrace this new story, and spend time getting acquainted with it, feeling it. Describe it out loud to yourself as your new emerging story. Write out the description of your new story in your journal. How can you integrate this new narrative into your life? Think of a symbol that represents your new story that you can bring into your life as a reminder of this relationship with money.

After writing your new money story, do something kind for yourself: make a cup of tea, take a short nap, take a walk, and acknowledge yourself and the benefits of attending to your own money story.

Affirmations

- I recognize and realize the Power and Presence at the center of my being.
- I honor my ability to create my new story.
- I'm excited to bring my new story into being.

Chapter 5
Women and Money

A feminist is anyone who recognizes the equality and full humanity of women and men.
—Gloria Steinem

For Women and Those Who Care about Women

Remember always that you as a woman, and the women you care for, are first a manifestation of Divinity. Women are beautiful creatives, visionaries, prophets, artists, geniuses, and marvels of every talent, gift, skill, and ability known to humankind.

As women, we have the blessings and the challenges of the blood mysteries of menstruation and menopause. We have bodies to honor for their sensuousness, and powerful passions that flow from our nakedness and our humanness. We have wombs to carry a baby and wombs to carry our creative endeavors, to birth them in the world with the same love, patience, caring, and protection we give our children. We have the magic in our bodies to create the milk to feed a baby—talk about a miracle! We, women, are birthers of life. We are manifesting the Divine by creating and celebrating our wisdom, our power, and our energy, honoring our Universal Source as we move in and through the world. I invite you to honor yourself as a woman with your whole self, your body, your mind, and your spirit.

In our Winter of money, let's reflect on our role as women.

Historical Perspective

Mythologically, the feminine is connected with life and death, fertility, and abundance. Early Sumerian, Egyptian, Greek, and Roman goddesses were all associated with coins, money, and fertility. Bernard Lietaer in *The Mystery of Money* asserts that water, cattle, milk, and women were all symbols of sustenance and nourishment for primitive societies, laying the foundation for the feminine as an expression of wealth and abundance.[7] With the ascent of the classical Greek, Roman, and Western civilizations, the honor, respect, and recognition of the great value of the feminine, of the Goddess, and of the role of women in society has diminished.

This is not a treatise or a historical essay on the demise of the feminine, or the fate of women in our society, just a reminder that the dishonoring of women happened. We know for example, that in ancient Sumer, the worship of the Goddess Inanna was replaced by the God Enlil of Nippur.[8] Later the Greek temple of Apollo replaced the Great Mother Temple of Delphi. Wikipedia offers this: "The Delphic oracle may have been present in some form from 1400 BC, in the middle period of Mycenaean Greece (1600–1100 BC). There is evidence that Apollo took over the shrine with the arrival of priests from Delos in the eighth century, from an earlier dedication to Gaia."[9]

We live with this history of Greek, Roman, and Western[10] thought that has given us logical thought, philosophy, mathematics, and reasoning. With the coming of monotheism, Judaism, Islam, and Christianity, the role of women was defined by religion. This religion was composed, written, translated, recorded, codified, taught, and interpreted by men since the beginning of recorded history. Through the use of the Torah, the Bible, scripture, and sacred writings, modern Judaism and Christianity, and more, Western society was shaped by the fact that only males were allowed to serve this male version of God.

Only males could be clergy, ministers, rabbis, priests, or preachers. Only males could conduct rituals, preside, and enter the holy places of the temples or churches. They were the educated, elite teachers, considered holy men, the rabbi, the priest, the minister, and the master with no concomitant words of honor for women in society. The creation story based on the Bible was a paradise where humanity was driven out because of a woman (Eve). If one were to look at native African, Central America, South American, or Native American creation stories, they are the opposite. In these creation stories, people were born into paradise, not cast out. Their Creators were often female, feminine, and worshipped because of their fertility. How different might our worldview be if women, fertility, and nature were celebrated, and paradise was our home?

Historically, the roles of women in the ancient world as oracles, priestesses, temple prophetesses, dancers, scribes, and healers were forbidden, marginalized, demonized, or eliminated over time. The worship of goddesses was considered an abomination or idol worship by the Jewish and Christian sects. Our history points to the witch hunts of early modern Europe beginning in the fifteenth and early sixteenth centuries, which continued for three-hundred years until the 1800s.[11] Most of these witch hunts targeted women. This is a tragic and deplorable episode of our human history. It's also telling that society as a whole found it acceptable treatment for those who did not follow the church-appointed decrees. Over time, if we relate the treatment of Mother Earth to the treatment of women, we can see that exploitation, abuse, denigration, or misappropriation define our capitalistic treatment of the Earth.

The history of the Judeo-Christian philosophy has a long arm into our modern society. My friend Michelle tells her story of growing up in the Midwest in the 1980s: "I grew up in a Primitive Baptist Church. It was *very* traditional. We used the old King James Version of the Bible. The men and women sat on opposite sides of the church. Even when we were eating together, the men would always discuss biblical passages. But the women could not talk." The effects of this history still pervade our society. My own story bears out that same oppression. I grew up in the Roman Catholic Church. Even today, there are no women at the altar in Roman Catholic churches (except altar girls who have been allowed since 1994). There are women in the pews, and women who answer the phone, clean the church, organize the parish activities, and teach the children. But women cannot lead mass, consecrate the Eucharist, baptize babies, anoint the dying, or proclaim the scriptures. The Roman Catholic Church continues to exclude one-half of the population based on gender! Meaning again, in our modern society, that maleness is equal to godliness and women are not worthy. I find it fascinating that society is willing to ignore one-half the world's capacity, talent, intelligence, skill, and genius solely based on one's physical anatomy. It's time for a change, don't you think?

I find it fascinating that society is willing to ignore one-half the world's capacity, talent, intelligence, skill, and genius solely based on one's physical anatomy.

Women and Money in the United States in This Century

In 1776, Abigail Adams sent a letter to her husband John Adams at the Continental Congress admonishing him, "I desire you would remember the ladies and be more generous and favorable to them than your ancestors."[12] However, it wasn't until over seventy years later in 1848 that the first Women's Rights Convention was organized. That same year, New York passed the Married Women's Property Act, allowing women to own property in their own name, enter into contracts, receive an inheritance, and not be liable for their husband's debts.[13] Many other states followed suit, using the New York law as a model.

Women in the United States were finally given the right to vote in 1920 after one hundred years of effort, with the passage and ratification of the 19th Amendment. In 1938, the Fair Labor Standards Act came into effect, creating a federal minimum wage and overtime pay, prohibiting child labor, and eliminating pay differences for men and women for hourly jobs. Although we would like to think everything is equal, we know that it is not. For example, "The formal sector consists of the businesses, enterprises and economic activities that are monitored, protected and taxed by the government, whereas the informal sector is comprised of the workers and enterprises that are not under government regulation."[14] Women have generally participated more in the informal economy through activities such as unpaid caregiving, especially of children and elders, volunteering, unpaid domestic work, unpaid family work, assisting other family members with their paid work, or subsistence work such as gardening, farming, or taking care of animals. In a fascinating article by GlobalCitizen.org, author Leah Rodriguez says, "Women and girls undertake more than three-quarters of unpaid care work in the world."[15] If women are marginalized or don't have access to the formal economy, there are consequences. As a stay-at-home mom, my professional opportunities for high-paid, professional work were limited. The opportunity to contribute economically to the Social Security system for retirement was limited. For example, my retirement savings are a fraction of my husband's. I earned a tiny portion of what my husband earned during his professional life. Yes, I raised my kids, kept the house, homeschooled for a time, volunteered, connected with family, gardened, and learned herbal medicine and homeopathy. But I didn't get paid for my efforts. My opportunities to learn new skills or continue my education are paid for by me personally, not by a company needing my skills.

Many women I know have issues that feel particular to women. It's almost like we have been taught to fear money, and to feel stupid or incompetent around money. We have been told we don't know how to make money, have money, or invest money. There is almost an expectation of hardship, struggle, or lack of money. There is also the exclusion of women from the paid labor force while we provide enormous and essential care for the young and old in our society. There is also the very real experience of not being invited into the "Good Old Boys Network," of being excluded from the boardroom, the golf course, or the conversations about money. As women, it is time to give ourselves permission to participate fully in finance and money decisions.

How many of us have heard the story, "I remember my mother's name on the checkbook as Mrs. Arturo Armijo" or "People knew my mom as Mrs. Harold Williams." Or the story, "Nobody taught me about money. My parents expected me to get married, have kids, and I would be taken care of by my husband." My friend Sofia tells the story, "In the 1960s, my mother, who was the breadwinner in our family, could not get a loan or a credit card for her business without her husband's signature." Another frequent story I hear is, "I was told that rich people are bad or that money is bad, so I never was supposed to want or need money, so why learn about it?"

Generally speaking, most of us are not taught about money. Often, we were sheltered from money discussions by our parents. Schools did not teach money management or financial literacy. Perhaps we have been told, "You are not allowed to talk about money." Or, there's also the "There, there sweetie, I'll take care of you," by the man, financial adviser, or banker. There is a money myth that we need to leave money to the "experts." As adults, women are often expected to know this foreign financial language (without being taught). Some women have a natural talent for money management, but the majority of us, me included, have had to learn slowly, often painfully, trying hard to navigate a system that is not feminine-friendly.

Globally, there are even bigger challenges for women. These include a lack of financial inclusion, access to credit, the digital divide, the unequal division of labor, and limited access to educational opportunities. Perhaps in our efforts to improve our personal money situation, we can improve the circumstances for women globally.

We know that women are financially active and impactful. "Whether they are single or partnered, women are making 90% of the financial decisions in American households."[16] It's also interesting and important to note that in the next few years, with the wealth transfer between generations, "Women will hold over $110 Trillion in Assets by 2025."[17] Historically, women have not had access to power or capital; fortunately, that is changing. Now is a good time to look at ways to remember we are global citizens, responsible for taking care of our world by using some of that money to fund clean energy, eliminate poverty, clean up the ocean, and mitigate climate change.

In a report by Age Wave and Merrill Lynch Wealth Management in 2017, they found that although women and men are equally confident in financial tasks such as paying bills and budgeting, women lack confidence when talking about investing. "There's a social taboo around talking about money that adds to the lack of confidence. 61% of women would rather talk about their own death than money. And 45% of women say they do not have a financial role model." [18] The report also shows that the media does not contribute to a healthy conversation about money or investing options. For example, in a review of 1,594 pages of editorial content in the March 2018 issues of the top seventeen women's magazines, there were only five pages covering personal finance. Additionally, the report found that the financial services industry catered to men with wealth-planning models based on men's salaries, life spans, and career paths. Another example is the retirement calculators which do not factor in planned or unplanned breaks in the workforce, which women more frequently take to raise children or care for aging parents.

Women and Investing

Investing is a deep and powerful area of concern and worry for many women. Women traditionally have less to invest due to a variety of circumstances. Women traditionally have been excluded from the investing world and shuttled off to the sidelines, so we are more likely to feel incompetent and fearful about money. The good news is that "women outperform men when investing."[19]

Money isn't everything for women, we know that. Family is a priority; seventy-seven percent of women say they see money in terms of what it can do for their families. Women care deeply about their families, their communities, and their causes. Women also give more of their income to charity. "Women at virtually every income level are more likely to give to charity and to give more money on average than their male counterparts, after controlling for education, income, and other factors that influence giving, new research from the Women's Philanthropy Institute (WPI) at the Center on Philanthropy at Indiana University finds."[20]

United Nations Sustainable Development, Goal 5: To Achieve Gender Equality and Empower All Women and Girls

Why is it important to know about the United Nations Sustainable Development Goal 5: To Achieve Gender Equality and Empower All Women and Girls? How does this factor into our thinking about money? Because, using money as a tool, and changing our money paradigm to Us, We, and the Earth, we need to be concerned and active about gender equality. "Empowering women and girls in developing countries ranked second among 76 solutions for curbing global warming to 2 degrees Celsius, according to a new report by the climate research organization Project Drawdown. Drawdown estimates that girls' education and family planning would reduce carbon by 85 gigatons by 2050."[21]

"Gender equality is not only a fundamental human right, but a necessary foundation for a peaceful, prosperous and sustainable world."[22] Gender equality has deep global significance. It impacts so many of the United Nations Sustainable Development Goals. It influences how women and girls are thought of, treated, and involved with society socially, politically, and economically.

There has been progress over the last decades: more girls are going to school, fewer girls are forced into early marriage, more women are serving in parliament and positions of leadership, and laws are being reformed to advance gender equality.

Despite these gains, many challenges remain: discriminatory laws and social norms remain pervasive, women continue to be under-represented at all levels of political leadership, and one in five women and girls between the ages of fifteen and forty-nine report experiencing physical or sexual violence by an intimate partner within a twelve-month period.[23] The situation with COVID-19 continues to negatively affect women and families. Perhaps the COVID-19 pandemic could provide opportunities to remedy inequalities and build a healthier and more inclusive world.

"The UN Sustainable Development Goal 5 includes the following targets:

- 5.1 End all forms of discrimination against all women and girls everywhere
- 5.2 Eliminate all forms of violence against all women and girls in the public and private spheres, including trafficking and sexual and other types of exploitation

- 5.3 Eliminate all harmful practices, such as child, early and forced marriage and female genital mutilation
- 5.4 Recognize and value unpaid care and domestic work through the provision of public services, infrastructure and social protection policies and the promotion of shared responsibility within the household and the family as nationally appropriate
- 5.5 Ensure women's full and effective participation and equal opportunities for leadership at all levels of decision-making in political, economic and public life
- 5.6 Ensure universal access to sexual and reproductive health and reproductive rights as agreed in accordance with the Programme of Action of the International Conference on Population and Development and the Beijing Platform for Action and the outcome documents of their review conferences
- 5.A Undertake reforms to give women equal rights to economic resources, as well as access to ownership and control over land and other forms of property, financial services, inheritance and natural resources, in accordance with national laws
- 5.B Enhance the use of enabling technology, in particular information and communications technology, to promote the empowerment of women
- 5.C Adopt and strengthen sound policies and enforceable legislation for the promotion of gender equality and the empowerment of all women and girls at all levels."[24]

These are important points for all of us to consider. We are sisters to the world, the poor, the women of color, the young, and the old. What we do with our thoughts, our lives, and our money matters, to us and to women of the world. By focusing on UNSDG Goal 5, we help all women and their families prosper.

As women and for women (and the larger society), we have an opportunity and a responsibility to shed the old paradigm (women have no value or are unworthy or undeserving) and create a new paradigm that aligns with the idea of an economy and a financial system that is just and inclusive and creates a society that works for all. We all must see women as sacred, grace-filled, and a full manifestation of the Divine.

As women, it's important to recognize the paradigm or thinking model we use when making money decisions. The old model of *Me, More, Mine*, about scarcity, accumulation, competition, power, and greed no longer works and should no longer define us.

The old model of *Me, More, Mine*, about scarcity, accumulation, competition, power, and greed no longer works and should no longer define us.

But we need to continue to remind ourselves of the new, inclusive paradigm. This template includes an ideal focus on community, cooperation, sufficiency, sustainability, and a recognition of the gifts, talents, and abundance that is not based on the dollar. It's time we incorporate the *Us, We, and the Earth* in our thinking, our incomes, expenses, investments, and finances so we can create a new reality of justice, kindness, and inclusion. It is an opportunity to see a bigger frame with a wider lens; it's a doorway to another kinder, more compassionate reality for caring for ourselves, each other, and the Earth, that I invite you to consider.

Woman as a Manifestation of The Divine

This is a short ritual to honor yourself as a woman or participate in honoring a woman.

Preparation: Bring a mirror and a card with the affirmations below. If you are inclined, light a candle or arrange a space with flowers.

Hold your card with the affirmations and send appreciation to your physical self, giving thanks for the marvels and beauty of your physical, emotional, and mental body. Hold the mirror and allow yourself to appreciate and honor who you are by saying the following affirmations.

Prepare a card with these affirmations:

- ❖ *I acknowledge me.*
- ❖ *I approve me.*
- ❖ *I applaud me.*
- ❖ *I accept me.*
- ❖ *I appreciate me.*
- ❖ *I am a beautiful manifestation of God/Goddess (or as you define).*

Prayer: *I am this amazing body. This body is a physical manifestation of the Sacred, the Holy, and the beautiful, created in the body of a woman. To you, Beloved, I come to rest. Bless my breath, my breasts, my belly, my brain, and my blood. Bless my womb, my creativity, and my genius. Bless my hands, my feet, my eyes, my lips, my hair. Bless my heart, my voice, my thoughts, and my prayers. I embrace my unique self, and my beautiful body, and give thanks for this mystery of life.*

Conclude by placing the affirmation card in a special place to remind yourself that you are a manifestation of the Divine.

End of ritual.

Affirmations

- ❖ My body is beautiful, a true manifestation of Divine Wisdom.
- ❖ Being a woman is a joy and a gift.
- ❖ I acknowledge, approve, accept, and appreciate myself and my efforts.

Part Three
Spring

Spring! Oh my, there are so many beautiful words and ways to describe spring: birthing, blooming, budding! It is a time of new life, planting, and the awakening of the Earth after the frozen winter. It's fresh, new, fertile, and alive. It's a wonderful time to plant new seeds and new intentions. We shake off the dense, gray, cold of winter and pay attention to the changing light as the Sun shines more each day, bringing warmth, brightness, and hope back to us and the Earth.

Hope can be hard to find in the barrenness of the dark. During the early spring, as winter relaxes its grip, there's a lightening, a softening, and a stirring of newness. Sap rises in the trees, and the daffodils and crocus arise from the dark rich soil. In our Spring of money, we begin to create new thoughts, new dreams, new life.

Many of the creation myths and stories speak of the light that is born from the darkness, or a people, a god or goddess emerging from the void. Spring is upon us, plants begin their blooming and budding cycle, sparrows and geese begin their courting, and the Earth is pregnant with expectancy and rich with possibility. Spring is the season when new life emerges from the Earth, spring rains dance with the fertile Earth to propagate new life in the form of leaves, blossoms, and babies of all sorts: lambs, caterpillars, and chicks. Spring is primal and restorative, an opportunity to say *yes!* to the new, to dance in celebration of new possibilities, and clean the cobwebs of winter from your house, your relationships, and yourself. Spring celebrates the last of winter's cold; light grows stronger each day. It's a time of renewal, a time of assessing the situation and clearing out the old ways of Winter. Spring is a time to plant our seeds of intention. When planting a lilac bush, it will not become a palm tree; when you plant corn, you don't expect to grow radishes. Spring requires preparation of the soil, and the seeds, sowing in the creative soil of your being, allowing those intentions to sprout and making sure you don't pull them up before they have time to grow and mature. It takes time to do this work.

In Chapter 6, we look at the history and influence of money and enoughness. In Chapter 7, we explore financial literacy and your current situation, looking at the nitty-gritty details of your financial life. We begin by looking at your income and expenses, your balance sheet and net worth, and examine debt and credit. In Chapter 8, we set our intentions, plant the seeds, and start our gratitude practice. What do you want to get out of this time and focus on money? What kind of relationship do you want to have with money? What is the life you want to lead and the legacy you want to leave behind? Together, in the Spring of money, we will be preparing the soil and planting the seeds of your new money life.

Spring Ritual

Choose a time to do your Spring ritual, even if it is not yet spring in your world. This is about planting seeds of intention and blessing your money with meaning.

Preparation: Gather a candle and lighter, incense, paper, and pen to write your intentions for this time and for your money. You may want to beautify your space with spring flowers or an offering of libations to share with the Earth. Bring two or three items that represent money or wealth to you. You can use your wallet, checkbook, dollars, your tax return, bank statements, financial statements, or any symbol of money. Choose items you want to honor as part of your financial path. Choose items that represent your intention to grow, expand, nurture, or nourish your money healing and your money plan. Prepare a space for your ritual, place your items on the Earth or a cloth, and light your candle. Sit in silence for one to five minutes (time yourself if necessary).

Opening : Honoring the Directions

> *I welcome the Blessings of the East, of Air, of New Beginnings. May I bring the winds of change to create a just, sustainable world.*
>
> *I welcome the Blessings of the South, of Fire, of Passion to light my spiritual fire to create a just, sustainable world with my life and my money.*
>
> *I welcome the Blessings of the West, of Water, of Wisdom, wash me clean, and open me to forgiveness of myself and others.*
>
> *I welcome the Blessings of the North, of Earth, of Sustenance, I honor and treasure your generous gifts of life and recognize the need to respect and protect our beautiful Mother Earth.*

Setting Your Intention: *Today my intention is to integrate my money, my financial resources, and my place in the world, with my soul and my commitment to a just, sustainable, thriving world.* Write your intentions in your journal.

Purification: Use incense or sage to cleanse your space and your energy. A lovely way to celebrate spring is to use a small bouquet of flowers dipped in fragrant water to spritz yourself and your space.

Ritual Blessing of Money

Pick up one of your financial items at a time, hold it to your heart and allow yourself time to own the role this item holds in your life. Think about how you want to move forward with what this item represents. Honor the relationship you have with this part of your financial life. Acknowledge the feelings and sentiments which arise. Remember the intentions you have for this part of your money journey. Bless each item, give thanks for the role it plays in your life, and give gratitude for this time to be with yourself, your soul, your Divinity, and your sacred money. When you have finished, allow yourself time to sit quietly; perhaps journal these experiences.

(If you do this ritual with another person or a group, you may want to share your insights or inspirations.)

Now speaking out loud (even to yourself), name, claim, and plant your seeds of intention for moving forth into your new money journey. You might say "*Infinite Source, I plant these seeds of intention, for (name your intention), I now allow these intentions, in the right time and in the right way to unfold with Divine guidance and wisdom.*"

Closing the ritual

> *Great Spirit, Source of all blessings, in thanksgiving I stand before You. I ask for Your guidance, Your counsel, and Your blessings. I again place my intention to honor You in all my decisions, to give thanks for the abundance, financial blessings, and amazing ways I am blessed. Blessed be. And so it is.*

Chapter 6
Money, History, and You

I can't paste it on me, it won't make me better looking, but sitting under a full moon, I have everything I need.
—Conscious Money Student

Money, Money, Money

Money in our society is mostly a transactional or impersonal exchange. It seems to me there's no heart, caring, or love in the world of money. I think it's time to bring a thoughtful, sensitive attitude to how we think about and use our money. It is certainly an interesting, human-generated, social construct that deeply influences our life and the world around us. Money fuels the local, national, and global economies. Historically, all types of items have been used as a medium of exchange, such as precious metals, salt, rice, corn, cacao beans, coffee, beads, and tobacco. As of 2022, the United Nations recognizes 180 currencies as legal tender. It is found in coins, paper, and digital forms including bitcoin and cryptocurrencies.[25]

The origin of the word *money* is the Latin root word *moneta* meaning mint or coin. In the center of ancient Rome stood the citadel overlooking the city. It was there the goddess Juno Moneta was honored in her temple and the first Roman coins were minted. In Greek tradition, she was also the goddess Hera. Recognizing the sacredness of money, coins, and protection of precious metals, the temple grounds were consecrated to the goddess who was also honored as the Queen of Heaven. She was considered the Great Mother of money, commerce, sacred marriage, and fertility among other epitaphs. Historically money is rooted in the feminine: in a goddess.

In India, the Hindu goddess Lakshmi is revered as the goddess of wealth, power, and prosperity. She is sometimes referred to as the Goddess of Gold. She is an expansive goddess of earth, moisture, and good fortune. Indian shopkeepers keep an image of this beautiful goddess who is usually depicted wearing red and gold, standing on a lotus blossom, gold coins pouring from her hands. These goddesses are examples of honoring wealth, abundance, and the Divine connection to our human existence. They are also beautiful symbols of feminine power and authority.

Historically and currently, gold and silver coins are symbols of wealth. Gold has always been associated with wealth and prosperity; it's expensive, rare, and has traditionally been used by rulers and monarchs as symbols of royalty. Gold, frankincense, and myrrh were gifts given to the Christ child in the Bible stories. Additionally, gold has long been associated with the round disk of the sun or the Sun as the Sky God.

Silver has been mined by humans since 3000 BCE. It has played an integral part in fueling human civilization. It is a beautiful metal, holding both the dark and the light. It can seem gray, but it can shine and reflect the beauty of shining silver in coins, jewelry, art, and sacred objects. Silver also corresponds with the beautiful disk of the full moon and her beautiful feminine energy.

Consciousness

What is consciousness? The Merriam-Webster Dictionary defines consciousness as:

> A: the quality or state of being aware especially of something within oneself.
>
> B: the state or fact of being conscious of an external object, state, or fact.
>
> C: awareness, especially concern for some social or political cause.

Another definition: that which is created in the mind before it manifests into reality. For example, an architect creates a drawing in her mind before she puts it on paper or into the computer system. Then, it can be constructed from those plans. But first comes the awareness of the need to create. Then we plant our seeds into the fertile soil of action, individually and collectively, to create a new world.

Awareness is one of the most powerful characteristics of conscious money and conscious life. When we are aware, we can consider options and opportunities instead of just doing things out of habit, circumstances, or conditioning. Our reflections of Winter create the awareness of Spring. We may wish to change a situation, but without thoughtful awareness, we can fall into old patterns or unhelpful tendencies.

When we talk about money, certainly our personal money, a fundamental part of making good decisions is knowing what we want our outcome to be. We may want to save $400 a month, but daily Starbucks, eating out three nights a week, and a $95 trip to the mall could derail those plans quickly. Bringing coffee from home, cooking at home, and wearing that beautiful blue sweater you bought on your last shopping spree may be easier if you have an awareness of what you want, your goal, and the outcome you are desiring.

We also associate powerful traits and qualities with the word *money*. Words such as *fear*, *dirty*, *lack*, *greed*, and *scarcity*. We also associate words such as *commerce*, *business*, *markets*, *budgets*, and *inflation* with money. In our society, wealth and self-worth are often considered the same. Does your bank account balance really define your value? Of course not. However, much of our society tells us that we are only as valuable as the amount of money we possess. If we look more deeply, we see we are valuable, just because we exist, just because we live. Further, money is just one of the resources available to us. The resources of community, caring, collaboration, and communication can enhance all of our intentions toward money.

However, much of our society tells us that we are only as valuable as the amount of money we possess. If we look more deeply, we see we are valuable, just because we exist, just because we live.

Currency moves through our society, through our economic system. It might be considered the lifeblood of our commercial and financial systems. Like everything in our universe, money is energy. It is a societal force that we have collectively agreed has value. I agree, money has value and can be used and channeled with love or hate, generosity or greed, with grace or with force, with forethought or carelessness. My hope and goal are that we together can use it in positive, beneficial ways that serve the greater good. Being conscious of our money is part of turning our money story around and changing our money paradigm. Using my money in a conscious, thoughtful way helps remind me that I am not a consumer, or a money machine, but rather a steward of my financial resources, and I can do this with a caring heart and a healthy relationship with my money.

My Spring Story

As a stay-at-home mom, I always had a part-time professional job. I worked as an assistant professor at a local university. I worked as an executive director at a national organization dedicated to promoting women's ordination in the Roman Catholic Church. I had a consulting practice doing nonprofit strategic planning. I went to school for naturopathy and homeopathy. I opened a small naturopathic practice. During that time, it seemed to me that my family did not see me in a role as a professional woman. My father, in particular, could not talk to me or ask me about my work. He could talk for hours about and with my brothers and their work. He would ask my brothers and my husband about their professional lives, their business dealings, and their activities outside the home. It was very painful for me that my own father couldn't recognize me as anything except a daughter, wife, and mother. The message I received was that my role was to be a daughter, sister, and mother; nothing else about me mattered.

After I married, I handed over the money decisions to my very smart, very kind husband. It's what I had been taught to do. As a stay-at-home mom, I didn't make much money. He took care of all the earnings, bills, taxes, and investments. My primary role and responsibility was to take care of our four precious boys and to do that as economically and sensibly as possible. My primary objective was to spend the least amount of money possible and still take care of our family.

During that period of my life, money was a challenge for both my husband and me. While we had money to raise our family because of my husband's work, we did not communicate well about money, how to spend, save, or invest it. He had his view, story, and inclinations, and I felt inept and inadequate to have meaningful conversations about money because I would get emotional, overwhelmed, or angry. It was a long process to heal my emotional triggers about money and finally be able to have honest and significant money conversations together.

When I started my money journey back in 2013, I needed to teach myself money basics. I did financial literacy courses. I bought books on money and finance. I noted the websites and resources I found online. I started a file on my computer that I titled Conscious Money. In April 2013, my husband and I attended a Slow Money Conference[26] in Boulder, Colorado. It was a wonderful introduction to socially responsible investing, investing in food, farms, and Earth-based communities. It sparked my interest in how to use my money in a more socially responsible, sustainable way. There were conversations, talks, and presentations about supporting families, farms, food, and soil with patient, slow investments. I learned about local investing, sustainable food production, investment clubs, and slow food. It was inspiring, informative, and exciting.

Upon my return, I rededicated my efforts to learn more about money. I began having conversations about conscious investing. One of the things we did on our return from Boulder was to find a socially responsible investment firm. We moved our retirement funds from a large investment management firm to a locally owned, woman-led company. We filled out all the paperwork and had meetings so she could understand our objectives and we could understand her strategies. I felt empowered to ask questions, learn more about investing, propose my ideas, and find a new focus for our money besides just growth and preservation. We wanted to have impact with our investments.

I figured out how to read financial statements and do due diligence. I explored financial organizations and focused on a regenerative economy. I learned about community capital, supporting local businesses, public banking, and investment clubs. Eventually, we moved our money completely out of the stock market into a Self-

Directed IRA. It was now up to us to direct our money and our investments. Our focus is our local community and projects that have a social impact. For example, when our friend Josephine fell ill, she missed one house payment. After that, she had late fees and higher interest. We were able to help her refinance her home and reduce her payment. This process has unfolded opportunities that have motivated me to heal my money story, to change my relationship to money, and use my money to help create a just, sustainable world.

Enoughness

You are enough. You are the breathing, acting, powerful manifestation of Divine expression. Being aware of your oneness with life, with nature, is a reminder that you are enough. Even though society, work, family, social media, and most marketing tell us we are inadequate, deficient, and incomplete, our job is to remember that fundamentally we are Divine Light, a manifestation of Spirit in physical form, and we are uniquely designed to offer our specific gifts and talents to the world. When we constantly criticize, compare, or lack confidence, we can feel like we are not enough—not doing enough, not good enough, not smart enough. These thoughts cause us to feel unbalanced and inadequate. When we think there is not enough, there is a tendency to hoard; there is mistrust, lack of communication with others, and fear.

Truthfully, we want what money provides, not money itself. We want to feel secure. We want to *feel* like we have enough. We want to *know* that we can care for ourselves and those we love. Money gives us the freedom to engage with the world, to create, and to participate with others. We want the flexibility and opportunities that money provides. We want to know we have the resources, the security, and the support that money can provide. We want to take care of others, to gift from our abundance, and to share generously with those we love.

Enoughness is the light of Spring returning to the world. It's our basis for hope. We will explore what it means to have enough, to recognize sufficiency, to find the full measure of richness and not just financial riches. We recognize that there are other equally important factors in our life: relationships, health, work, and our connection to Spirit.

A central tenet to all spiritual work is that you are sacred, complete, and whole just as you are right now. You are enough. This journey is personal and based on your own history. By healing those old stories of fear, incompleteness, or lack of worth, you heal the world.

While writing this book, I was scheduled to be with some of my family for a gathering. When certain individuals did not show up, I was quite triggered. I reached out to a friend to talk it over. She helped me recognize that I was wanting my family to acknowledge me, affirm me, to appreciate me. But after a long conversation, I realized that I am the one who needs to acknowledge, affirm, and appreciate myself. No one can do that for me. Many of us do not get the approval, acceptance, or acclaim we deserve. That is the way of the world. What matters is that you approve and appreciate yourself. By declaring that you are enough, that you have all you need to be you and move and live in this world, you can rest from continually needing or seeking more. That same approach works for money. Right here, right now, at this moment, there is enough.

In her book, *The Soul of Money*, Lynne Twist identifies three toxic myths of scarcity:[27]

- There is not enough.
- More is better.
- That's just the way it is.

There is a societal myth—a myth of scarcity—that *there's not enough:* there is not enough food, enough water, enough time, or enough money. This fear drives us to plan and organize our lives to make sure we get our share. The second myth Twist presents is that *more is better*. It is part of the old paradigm of *Me, More, Mine.* It focuses on external successes instead of the inner gifts and resources that are available to us. Finally, Twist suggests the myth of *that's just the way it is.* This myth presents us with an excuse for the way the world works; it may not be just, kind, sustainable, or even reasonable, but that's how it is. These myths are so prevalent that we seem to swim in them like fish who don't even know they are in the water. These myths undermine our courage and determination to see ourselves and our world as enough.

You are enough. That's the foundation of working with money in the world. For now, recognize the lovely enoughness that exists in your life. You have the wisdom and the spark within yourself for this journey. It is a spiritual process, a course of action for your money and your checkbook but mostly for your soul. You are complete and whole, just as you are, right here, right now.

You are complete and whole, just as you are, right here, right now.

EXERCISE

I Am Enough

Get your journal and write a paragraph about enoughness in your life. Then list five places in your life where you feel that you have enough, are enough, or there is enough. Then next to each item, write why it is enough. Note the insights of what makes you feel like there is enough. Notice the gratitude that arises when we appreciate the enoughness in our life.

Affirmations

- I am enough, right here, right now.
- I have everything I need within me: my vision, my power, and my determination.
- Opportunities and wonderful possibilities fill me with hope.

Chapter 7
What Matters Most—Setting Your Intention

True wealth is not measured in money or status or power. It is measured in the legacy we leave behind for those we love and those we inspire.
—César Chávez

Intention Setting

Planting the seeds is required to grow our intentions. If we don't know what we want from our life or our money, it is very hard to achieve the outcome we desire. Telling yourself that you want to "do better" or "have more money" is not a workable goal or intention, it's an idea that starts the process. It's a little bit like saying, "I want to build a house." Yes, it's an idea, but the details are not specific enough to see the task through to completion. It is vital to set an intention for money work.

I love Stephen Covey's admonition: "Begin with the end in mind." It's a reminder that if we don't know why we're doing something, then there's no point in doing it. We exercise, go to the gym, and take vitamins because we want a healthy body. We call our parents, send birthday cards, and schedule family reunions to stay in touch with family. We plan to go to Europe, complete a painting, remodel the kitchen, buy a new car, or start a business because we have the end in mind. Setting intentions about money is equally important. Plant the Spring seeds you want to see growing.

This chapter is about setting intentions for yourself, for your money, and for your life. Let's get more specific about what kind of relationship you want to have with money, the actions you propose to take, and the goals to which you aspire.

In her book *Activate Your Money*, Janine Firpo recommends a financial plan that includes these five requirements for building your wealth:

1. Spend less than you make.
2. Pay off debt.
3. Save.
4. Invest.
5. Monitor your investments.

By calculating your income and expenses, and working to stay within your income, in addition to seeing the numbers, it's comforting to know you are moving along in your money journey. By paying attention to debt, and making a plan to pay off your debt, you again, have this piece of your money journey and financial plan in place. Then, you can move on to set your money goals.

Lewis Carroll reminds us, "If you don't know where you are going, any road will get you there." There are stories of business giants and committed scientists who set goals and achieved them. There are workbooks, coaches, and business plans that outline goals. Goal setting helps you to define what you want to achieve; this is personal, and specific to you and your life. It also helps motivate you to commit to the difficult tasks that are always part of the goal. It's like a map of your personal treasure. But only you know what that treasure chest holds. Creating a goal based on other people's or society's expectations will not work. We live in a "more, bigger, better, faster" world. If you are building goals based on smaller, slower, and less is more, then you may be out of sync with the outside world but wonderfully connected to your deepest desires.

We all know there are reasons we don't set goals: we don't want to take the time, it's too hard, it's overwhelming, and of course, there is the fear that we won't really reach our goals. Understand that you are sacred. You are magnificent just the way you are, and by tapping into that Divinity, you can focus on yourself, your money, and your intention toward your best life.

There really is no limit to your personal self-expression. It will not look like anyone else's. By loving yourself, honoring your-self enough to do what is best for you and the way you choose to live, money is part of that plan.

Understand that you are sacred. You are magnificent just the way you are, and by tapping into that Divinity, you can focus on yourself, your money, and your intention toward your best life.

We know that money is actually a social construct. It's not just the dollar. It's the web of connections, people, business, feelings, and history. There are people who have an interest in your money. You may have family members who depend on you or business partners who have expectations. There are systems structured to support or suppress you: for example, banks, government organizations, or charities. How you feel about these relationships in your life, and how positive or stressful they are, will help you determine how you want to move forward with your money goals.

Finally, you can envision what you want your life to look like if you had sufficient capital to fund your ideal life. What is it you want for the most creative, enriching, grace-filled life you can imagine? Is it extravagant or simple? Ponder what would give you the deepest feelings of fulfillment. Don't forget art, music, your spiritual life, recreation, volunteering, philanthropy, and sharing your creative gifts with the world. What lifestyle is calling your name?

One of the definitions of wealth is the ability to afford and experience your most authentic self. Affluence can also be a feeling of abundant flow, appreciating the whole experience of living. Remember that you do have innate wisdom and a deep understanding of yourself and your money. Find the place inside you where you feel peaceful, content, grateful, and in your body. Perhaps you might go for a walk, do meditation, practice yoga, or work out at the gym to spark the energy to sit and ponder your life and money goals. Energy flows where intention and attention go. This is your time to rise up to be your biggest and best self, spiritually and financially.

Your Spiritual and Financial Legacy

Creating a legacy requires thoughtful consideration, a clear picture of what is important, and how you want to bless current and future generations. Think about things you are grateful for, proud of, and for which you would like to be remembered. Thinking deeply about what this means to you helps define how you create the life you want to live. It also helps define how you want to use, invest, and distribute your valuables, assets, and money when you die. If you are not ready to address these questions, perhaps taking care of today's business is the priority, and you can come back to your legacy focus later.

The other consideration, as you ponder these legacy questions, is the kind of world you want to leave for future generations. Remember the exercise in Chapter 4: Your Vision for a World That Works for All? What did you write in your money journal?

> What kind of legacy do you want to leave to your family, your community, and the world?

What inspires you to make decisions and choices that are meaningful to you? Have you considered your community, the global community? The Sustainable Development Goals[28] are wonderful guideposts for considering where to put time and resources. What kind of legacy do you want to leave to your family, your community, and the world?

Each of us has our personal history, traditions, heritage, family background, spiritual framework, education, and work history. We have experienced beauty, art, sports, music, travel, and nature. We have our hopes, our dreams, and our ideals. How do you want to share those now and with future generations?

Consider also how you want your estate to be distributed. How much of your estate do you want to give to heirs, other individuals, or philanthropic organizations? As you think about how you want to use your money today, how can you put money in place to contribute to a just, sustainable future?

Estate planning is a process, one that many of us have not yet completed. It feels like a big task, and often we do not know where to start or what to do. If we die "intestate" (that is, without a legal will), settling the estate will be done in court, and no one will have a say in how the estate will be distributed. Of course, we know we should make a will, but there are several other tasks that should also be put in place, so your survivors know how to attend to your wishes. An estate plan includes your last will and testament, your living will or your advance medical directives, a durable power of attorney, a list of your assets, and a letter of instruction for your estate administrator. Of course, there are other documents you may need, but this will get much of your estate in place. These documents need to be prepared and periodically reviewed. The site Investopedia.com has a great list called Estate Planning: 16 Things to Do Before You Die.[29] What action or actions will you take in the next thirty, sixty, or ninety days to prepare your estate plan?

EXERCISE

Financial Visioning

Sit quietly with your journal. Light a candle and ask yourself what you want your financially wise life to look like.

- What kind of person do you want to be personally and financially?
- What would you like to do, that until now, was not part of your ideal financial life?
- What emotions do you want to feel about your finances?
- What kind of legacy do you want to leave?

Take an hour each week over the next four weeks to brainstorm and prioritize your financial goals:

- Short-term goals (sixty to ninety days)
- One-year goals
- Five-year goals
- Long-term goals

Affirmations

- ❖ I am so pleased to step into my best financial life yet.
- ❖ I have all the guidance and wisdom I need within me.
- ❖ I am grateful to have a well thought out and prepared financial plan.

Chapter 8
My Spiritually Focused Financial Life

Money is a terrible master but an excellent servant.
—P. T. Barnum

Leticia moved to Phoenix from her small hometown in rural Arizona. She met Javier, who was out of work. She supported the two of them, putting most of their living expenses on her credit card. After two years and a miscarriage, she left the relationship. For three years, she paid the minimum amount of $25 on her credit card. The interest on her $7,800 balance was 24 percent. Finally getting the courage to address her finances, we looked at her income and her expenses. She addressed her money fears, and she made a decision to refocus on getting out of debt to move forward with her life. After seeing how minimum payments on her credit card would require seven more years of debt, she consolidated her debt and made a commitment to monthly payments which she was able to pay back in two years. By understanding her money situation and making a pledge to herself to be debt free in two years, she felt free to move on in her life. She moved to Dallas, met a new boyfriend, and addressed her money with courage.

Phebe left home at sixteen to live with an older boyfriend. She had no job, no money, and no experience with money. When she went to work as a performer, her manager-husband handled all the financial details of her life. Later, after marrying and having children, and getting divorced, she depended on her father for money support. It wasn't until her fifties, after her two daughters left home, that she was able to look at money, work on getting out of years of credit card debt and begin to make sense of her money. The shame and remorse about her years of not tending to her money were difficult. Now, she is making her own money, saving for retirement, and making mortgage payments on her dream home in the heart of the city.

As we address our financial life, I want to remind us that this financial life is part of who we are spiritually. The point of this work is that we are spiritual beings, having physical and financial experiences. Money is one of the tools in our toolbox.

Much of what we learn about money is through interactions with our family and personal history. Public schools teach academic information, but the practical aspects of finances, checkbook management, savings, and compound interest are usually not part of the curriculum. You may not have been taught these skills, but it's never too late to learn them. Consider taking a basic financial literacy course to learn the basics of money management.

I want to acknowledge that for many of us, money brings up feelings of chaos, worry, or fear. By noticing and recognizing those feelings in our body, and in our mind, we can address them. Ultimately, we can have order, clarity, and feel empowered. If you are feeling bewildered or confused, stop, and take good care of yourself. Suffering is not necessary on this journey, fear is not a necessity to organize your money, and staying stuck is optional.

Addressing your feelings is a good way to allow flow, both emotionally and with your money. As you become more confident and clearer, fear can be alleviated, and your relationship with money can and will improve. Insecurity makes way for balance. Financial freedom is possible, if we remember that money is not our source, but rather God, Goddess, or the Universe—however you define the Greater Good—is our Source. The Infinite is our source of well-being, our guidance in this process, and our creative self-expression. Money is just one facet of our life. If we can get it in order, it helps with all the other areas of our lives. Let's start with basic money management.

Financial freedom is possible, if we remember that money is not our source, but rather God, Goddess, or the Universe—however you define the Greater Good—is our Source.

We live in a complicated world, and money is only one piece of the very big puzzle called life. But unless you can find the pieces and put them in place, the puzzle isn't very fun or engaging, nor does it make sense. An important point is that baby steps allow us to move forward. We know that there are specific tasks, steps, or work we need to do. These are usually painful reminders, for example, an IRS letter, a bank overdraft notice, or a cousin you want to avoid because you owe her money. Addressing those things first, with compassion for yourself, begins the process. By taking time to clean out your financial closet and put things in order, you can make good financial decisions and create a healthy financial condition for yourself, your family, and the world.

There are a variety of financial management courses to help you learn basic financial management.[30]

Probably two of the best-known names in financial literacy are Dave Ramsey[31] and Suze Orman.[32] Both courses, along with many others, can walk you through taking charge of your finances. There are books, websites, online courses, step-by-step money management, wealth building, and investment programs. There are more options than ever before. There are money coaches, money therapists, money counselors, investment specialists, and the list goes on. Keep in mind too, that getting support from an accountant, CPA, or investment professional may be in your best interest. However, finding what you want, need, and what will work with your temperament as well as your budget can be tricky. But clarity is a wonderful thing. That's what cleaning out your financial closets is all about.

Just like that overfull hall closet or storage shed that hasn't been cleaned since you moved in, your financial closet requires periodic maintenance, cleaning, and maybe even renovation and remodeling. What worked in the past may not work anymore. Your inclinations in the past may not serve your goals for the future. Perhaps you haven't filed your taxes in three years. Maybe you still owe your parents the money you borrowed when you were in graduate school. Maybe you keep getting overdraft fees because you don't know how to balance your checkbook.

In order to move forward with a new dedication to aligning your money with your values, you need to tend not just to your history, emotions, and values, but also to the realities of daily money management.

I know the challenge of looking at numbers, tasks, and spreadsheets can be overwhelming. Go back to your centering tools, go for a walk to clear your mind, do a forgiveness session, forgive yourself for past mistakes, and use EFT to bring down your anxiety or release any distress you are feeling. Once you are calm, remember, this is about having a good relationship with your finances, and having good financial numbers makes life so much easier.

Income and Expenses

In a recent class, Lisa, a single mom of an active seven-year-old, carefully tracked her income and expenses for two months. It was a big insight when she realized she was often giving away money to her family because she didn't want to disappoint the people around her. With that insight, she was able to set boundaries and say no to these requests that didn't fit into her budget.

One easy way to begin to track your expenses is to carry a small notebook and write down every time you spend money. For example,

Wednesday

Lunch out $21.81

Notebook for journaling $5.28

Phone bill $181.11

Groceries $126.37

Vitamins $45.97

Coffee $5.56

Over time, this can be an eye opener! Are you spending five dollars a day on coffee or soda? Just being aware is always a first step to change.

Profit and Loss

The primary information you need to begin looking at your financial records is an income and expense statement, also known as a profit and loss or P and L, which tracks your income and expenses. Income is whatever brings in money and generally includes salaries, interest income, dividends from investments, and capital gains from the sale of stocks or bonds. Expenses are the outlay of money. Any item where there was an outflow of money is an expense. This can include rent, utilities, gas, food, and entertainment, as well as other expenses such as vacations or appliances. Tracking every expense is the not-so-fun part of financial accounting, but also a necessary part of cleaning your financial closet. By measuring your cash inflows and outflows, you can see if you have a positive net cash flow (meaning more income than expenses) or a negative net cash flow (meaning more expenses than income). It's often helpful to compare income and expenses over time, for example, this month with last month or this year in comparison to last year.

Credit

There are many definitions of the word *credit*, regarding money, but a simple definition is "the provision of money, goods, or services with the expectation of future payment."[33] Credit plays an important role both for individuals and businesses. The ability to borrow money easily allows the economy to move, grow, and change. A consumer credit system allows people to buy goods and services, without having to pay cash at the time of purchase. If you have good credit, you can more easily borrow money and get better terms or arrangements on payment options. Conversely, if you have bad credit, have old debt, or had difficulty making payments in the past, then lenders may be less likely to loan money. Often, they will charge higher interest or deny a loan, a credit card, or money for business expansion.

Your Credit Score—Why It Matters

Richard was trying to refinance his mortgage, but he needed to improve his credit score. He went to pull his credit report and the credit report said that he was deceased. It took months of work to correct the credit report. It was also months of higher interest on his home loan.

Do you understand your credit score? Have you checked it recently? Most credit scores range from 300 to 850. The higher the score, the easier it is for you to qualify for a loan or get a lower interest rate. Your credit score is based on information reported by lenders or creditors to the credit reporting companies. The three big companies are Equifax, Experian, and TransUnion. Take time to check your report with these companies and make sure your report is correct since mistakes on the report can hurt your credit score. You can get one free credit report from each of the three credit reporting companies every twelve months. The Consumer Financial Protection Bureau in the United States oversees credit reports.[34]

Debt

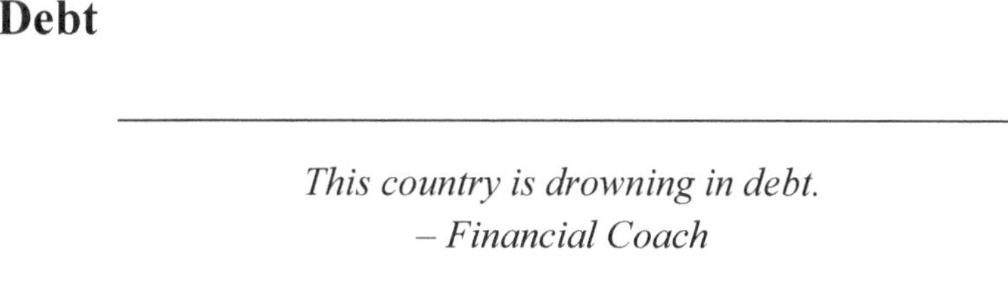

Terrance wanted a new truck for work and for upgrades on his five-acre plot of agricultural land. He also wanted to build his credit. So, he bought a brand-new Ford F-150. He arranged to make the payments over five years. Then he got behind on his payments, which meant he was paying higher interest and over time the amount owed on the truck was more than he could get by selling it. For Terrance, he owed $36,000 on a truck that was then worth $30,000. It's actually a common problem, sometimes described as "being upside down," or having "negative equity." In an article for CarProUSA, Jerry Reynolds recommends, "The way to avoid negative equity is to get a good deal upfront on what you are buying, put down 10% or more in cash or trade equity, get the best interest rate possible, and get the shortest loan period you can and be comfortable."[35] Terrance continued to make payments on his truck because that was the debt he owed.

Tomas and Veronica were deep in debt, to the tune of $30,000 owed to a variety of lenders, including payday lenders with interest rates over 400 percent. Each month they were short $1600 just for debt payments and regular expenses. Veronica had been working, but with the COVID pandemic, she stayed home with their eleven-year-old son. So, Tomas used payday loans to keep the family afloat. Veronica tried to stay out of being involved with those decisions; she didn't want to talk about money. There was stress, tension, and a lack of communication. When Tomas came to us for a conversation about debt consolidation, we talked about the need for them to discuss their financial situation. After a couple of conversations, we all came up with a debt consolidation plan and Tomas and Veronica began a new relationship with each other and a plan for their money that included a new spending plan, getting out of debt, and saving to buy a house.

The United States is a nation whose consumers have been instructed by advertising and credit card companies that we can have anything we want, any time we want, and we can pay for it later, on credit. This is why so many struggle with a very heavy burden of debt.

Consumer debt has many people locked in a prison that seems like it has no key. It is the bondage of the financial chains that shackle millions of people in the United States and around the world. We have been conditioned into thinking our social status and value are based on the logo, label, or status symbol and that we have to buy in order to have the status, respect, and reputation we desire.

If the issue of debt brings up emotions of powerlessness or victimhood for you, please remember to use the exercises in Chapter 6 to bring yourself back into balance. Also, be mindful that, regardless of your money situation or the amount of debt you have, you, at the core, are whole, complete, and a manifestation of the Divine here in this world.

Also, be mindful that, regardless of your money situation or the amount of debt you have, you, at the core, are whole, complete, and a manifestation of the Divine here in this world.

You are not a bad person because you have debt. There is a bigger mind, the mind of God, that allows us to release the fear, insecurity, and overwhelm of being in debt.

We all have bills: mortgages or rent, car payments, and credit cards. The other part of the equation is the unconscious use of credit for things we don't need or that we buy when we don't need them. In a society where "bigger, better, and faster" are the norm, getting a brand-new (bigger, better, faster) and more expensive (name the item of your choice) often happens because we don't consider the consequences.

Debt at the personal, as well as the social, level is omnipresent. In the second quarter of 2023, household debt was at $17.06 trillion, and credit card debt reached one trillion dollars.[36]

In his book, *Say Yes to No Debt: 12 Steps to Financial Freedom*, DeForest B. Soaries, Jr. says, "We've come to accept, as normal, a lifestyle in which we are always behind, borrowing from our future earnings to assuage our present bill collectors to pay for a forgotten past."[37]

Coming to terms with our own personal debt situation and taking time to make a plan to get out of debt is part of building a healthy relationship with money. I know from personal experience and from helping clients get out of debt, that there is freedom, relief, and independence when sizable portions of our money are not being allocated to the debt.

Debt Owed Me

Another challenge we often face is loaning people money. Perhaps they then never mention it again, or they say they will pay it, or pay only a portion. We are left behind, our money is gone, and the debt remains unpaid. Forgiveness tools, the EFT, and reaching out to have closure about the situation are all good ways to bring resolution to the situation.

Other Items in Your Financial Life

As you are arranging your finances, consider cleaning up the rest of your life documents. Allot one place where all this information is easily accessible and where at least one other person knows how to access this information.

Here is a checklist of items in your financial life that need to be organized and tended to.

- Bank accounts and online banking accounts
- Credit card accounts
- Mortgages
- Loans
- Insurance policies
- Tax returns
- Pension plans and retirement accounts
- Stock accounts and other investments
- Property titles or deeds
- Wills, trusts, and powers of attorney
- Advance directives
- List of professional help (attorney, CPA, insurance agent)

Banking and Budgets

In order to make a budget, you need to balance your bank account so you know how much money you have to work with. To keep your bank register accurate, make sure to include checks and withdrawals as well as deposits and income.

Once you know your monthly income and expenses, it's time to make a budget. There are plenty of budget sheets, Excel forms, and online budget apps. I highly recommend you find something you like that's easy to use and that is easily available. Below you will find a sample budget using the same categories we used for your income and expenses. Keep in mind, there is never a perfect budget or a perfect month. Things always come up, but categorizing your spending helps eliminate surprises and gives you a wider perspective on your money.

If you are in partnership, please engage kindly when discussing budgeting and cash flow. Perhaps you start by doing your budget alone, then talking with your partner. Or consider a regularly scheduled money date with your spouse. If things get intense or hard, take a break and come back later. Taking time to create a new relationship with money requires time, patience, and kindness toward yourself and others in your life. In her book *The Art of Money*, author and financial therapist Bari Tessler cautions us, "Money dates with your honey will take practice. Most of us were simply never taught how to have safe, compassionate, and playful money conversations with our partners, so it takes some time to open up lines of communication."[38] These conversations can be rough, emotional, and complicated, but remember, you are developing a new relationship with money and with each other in a fresh and transformative way.

EXERCISE

Financial Literacy

Find a financial literacy program, website, app, or book to support your journey. Consult the suggested resources at the end of the book. Commit to using your new support system weekly or daily if that works for you. Remember this is an adventure, with new horizons soon to be seen. It's an opportunity to see a new way with money, and to commit to using your money, time, and resources to create a just, sustainable world. Doing the work to put things in place is part of the process. Begin with the Income and Expenses Exercise below.

EXERCISE

Income and Expenses

Track your income and expenses for the previous two months and this current month. Compare the numbers and remember to take plenty of time for caring for yourself in this process.

Journal your insights about keeping track of your money. How do you feel about your relationship with money? What are a couple big areas in your financial life that need attention?

Write out three actions to take in the next month to manage your money more effectively than in the past.

Last Month

Income/Deposits

Total Income/Deposits

Expenses/Disbursements
Mortgage/Rent
Car Payments
Credit Card Payments
Student Loan Payments
Other Loan Payments
Childcare
Health Insurance
Life Insurance
Child Support
Alimony
Taxes
Utilities
Phones
Cable TV/WiFi
Groceries
Car Gas
Car Maintenance
Medical Dental
Clothing
Entertainmart
Eating Out
Education
Subscriptions
Dues/Memberships
Gifts/Contrubutions
Travel
Other Expenses

Total Expenses/Disbursements

Month Before Last

Income/Deposits

Total Income/Deposits

Expenses/Disbursements
Mortgage/Rent
Car Payments
Credit Card Payments
Student Loan Payments
Other Loan Payments
Childcare
Health Insurance
Life Insurance
Child Support
Alimony
Taxes
Utilities
Phones
Cable TV/WiFi
Groceries
Car Gas
Car Maintenance
Medical Dental
Clothing
Entertainmart
Eating Out
Education
Subscriptions
Dues/Memberships
Gifts/Contrubutions
Travel
Other Expenses

Total Expenses/ Disbursements

EXERCISE

Debt List

Do your body check in (see Tools in Chapter 1). Make a list of all the debts you owe. Bless all the items on your list. Sit with the feelings. Repeat the Debt Prayer, do the EFT or a forgiveness meditation to release feelings of overwhelm, victimhood, or shame.

Write out a plan of action. Choose one item to do immediately; for example, make an extra payment or pay off a loan. Remember your divine nature and your desire to connect your money with your values. Congratulate yourself on taking time to look at your debt situation.

Speak this prayer aloud:

> *Divine Guidance, I place my trust and faith in you. I claim peace and confidence to live and move and have my being, my money, and my debt be a path to you. I allow Divine Source to provide the right way and the right time to live debt free. I surrender all doubt, fear, and uncertainty. I give thanks for this gift of life.*
>
> *Or write this out on paper, post it on your bulletin board or set it on your altar.*

EXERCISE

Net Worth Calculation Worksheet

The next financial statement that you will work on is called a balance sheet. It's a snapshot of your financial position at a specific point in time. It is a statement of your assets, and liabilities, detailing the balance of income and expenses for a specific period of time. It is a summary of what you own (assets), and what you owe (liabilities) which then shows the difference between assets and liabilities (net worth). Assets can be cash, checking or savings accounts, homes, cars, real estate, and investments. Liabilities are what you owe, such as current bills, payments owed on some assets like cars or homes, credit card balances, taxes, and debt such as personal or student loans. Subtracting liabilities from your assets will give you your net worth. If you owe more than you own, it may be time to put a debt repayment plan in place. Net worth provides you with the information you need to put your financial plan in place. This process also allows you to have all your information in one location.

Every year, your net worth should be tabulated to review your progress and compare it with your financial goals. In addition, a net worth statement is a valuable aid in planning your estate and establishing a record for loan and insurance purposes.

Net Worth Calculation Worksheet

Assets -What you own

Cash

- On hand ____________
- In banks etc. ____________

Real Estate

- Home ____________
- Other ____________

Investments

- Brokerage accounts ____________
- Retirement accounts ____________
- Other ____________

Personal Property

- Vehicles ____________
- Home furnishings etc ____________
- Jewelry etc ____________
- Collections ____________
- Other

Total Assets ____________

Liabilities - What you owe

Current debt (less than 1 year)

- Credit cards ____________
- Medical ____________
- Other ____________

Mortgages

- Home ____________
- Other ____________

Other Debt

- Bank/finance company ____________
- Auto loans ____________
- Student loans ____________
- Other loans ____________

Total Liabilities ____________

Net Worth - Assets minus Liabilities [ ]

Affirmations

- ❖ I am so grateful to be here, honoring myself and my money.
- ❖ I am pleased to be working with the details of my financial life.
- ❖ I appreciate and approve of my work with money. I am inspired and engaged in this money process.

Part Four
Summer

Abundance is not something we acquire. It is something we tune into.
—Wayne Dyer

How magical summertime is!! It brings memories of vacations, sandcastles, running barefoot through the sprinklers, and the ice cream truck passing. The weather is hot, the BBQ grill sizzling, and the lake water cool. Fireworks delight us, the garden delivers its promised treasures. Summer extends the light and warmth to remind the blossoms, fruit, and berries to grow, to flourish. This is the creative and the creation phase of the year. It's a time of growth and expansion. It's when the tomatoes and zucchini overproduce. It's when things develop; there is headway and a surge of movement. It is a time to celebrate all we have accomplished, knowing that soon the light will begin to diminish, and the cycle of seasons continues.

Summer is the time of light, heat, and the power of the sun. It is the season of growth, production, performance, and making things happen. This can be the time you shine with your successes in your life and in your money work! Your garden is ripening, the seeds you planted are growing, and Mother Nature shares her magnificent and abundant largesse with you.

Sometimes we need to be reminded to take stock of our money blessings. Summer is a good time to remember and rejoice in our blessings, to see what we have accomplished!

Summer is HOT! Water yourself and your garden faithfully, and check for pests and diseases. As the temperature soars and you long to get out of the heat, the rain comes, as often do fires, burning, and lightning. It's a time to protect yourself and your precious plants. Summer is the season of fire and passion. Equally, it can be the season of the fury and destruction of hurricanes and tornadoes.

This applies to your money as well. To cultivate our seeds of intention, we need to care for and water them. But storms, winds, or crises can derail the best of intentions. Staying true to your intention for yourself and for your money is critical. Yes, be gentle and kind to yourself. Remember to rest, nourish yourself, and celebrate the smallest victories. The harvest is coming, but now is the season of growth and expansion. It's an opportunity to celebrate the power of the sun, fertility, and the abundance of living systems. It's also a reminder that we too have an inner fire, a radiant vitality: the Divine mystery which equips and empowers us to grow stronger physically, financially, and spiritually.

In this Summer section, we will talk in Chapter 9 about the role of work and money. In Chapter 10, we begin to do things differently by making conscious decisions about the impact of consumerism in our life and our world. We review our money relationship with work, the community, and the United Nations Sustainable Development Goals. In Chapter 11, we will look at our role in our consumer society as conscious consumers.

My Summer Story

When I decided to focus on money back in 2013, I had recently moved to Albuquerque to work and to be closer to my father, who was not well. My focus back then was social impact or socially responsible investing. I wanted our investment money to do some good in the world, rather than just sit in the stock market. We belonged to a local food cooperative that had a Social Investment Fund. With money from investors, local farmers could get a low-interest loan for things like seeds, new equipment, or moving more land into organic agriculture. I wrote my first $5000.00 check to that fund. Previously, my sweet husband handled all those types of financial transactions. I was so proud of myself. I was growing as a money steward and leaning into my discomfort. I read lots of articles and books, and I learned about social impact bonds, risk, liquidity, and ROI (return on investment). I learned about locovesting (investing locally), term sheets (which is a description of the conditions of an investment), and due diligence. My goal was to be responsible and literate about money.

One of my realizations about money was that the more I learned and the more familiar I became with both my personal spending and our financial situation, the less I felt so defeated or sad about money. I could finally have a conversation and feel okay about my questions and my baseline knowledge. This process was healing my relationships with my husband and with money. I knew I had more to learn, and I was pleased that I was making progress.

As I grew, I also had to recognize my own internal conflicts. I love beautiful things, vintage furniture, beautiful artwork, and expensive clothes. Beauty is important to me but spending lots of money on such things, when my larger goal is to create a just, sustainable world seems incongruent. I love to travel, but getting on an airplane with its concomitant carbon footprint when I am concerned about climate change presents an internal conflict. These ambiguities and contradictions in me are real and challenging. I want to do what's right; I also must consider my husband, my family, our community, and the global world. It's hard to reconcile all those aspects of life. However, learning to be kind and gentle with myself is always the first task (otherwise I can't be that way with others).

I will also say that part of growing spiritually is the ability to hold those contradictions with kindness and compassion. Learning to bear the ambiguity, inconsistencies, and challenges is part of life. We can do it gracefully, or we can do it awkwardly, but those paradoxes are fundamental to being human. The question is how to hold all that we, too, have inside of us. We are simultaneously both the light and dark within. There is knowing and not knowing; there is good and evil; there is the rose and the thorn; the honey and the bee sting.

Eventually, perhaps we can find the wisdom that allows us to see the contradiction, to include it all, and understand that everything belongs; yet in our own way, we can choose where to tend, give attention, and focus. That is our Summer work: to give care to what we want to grow and weed out what isn't right for our lives.

During this time of my money journey, I also began to see the connections with our societal view of economics. This view of being separated from Nature, the separation of the haves and the have nots, survival of the fittest, and a model of perpetual growth does not work for most of the world. It was time to look at the economics and relationship with our Earth and with our community. I heard about the Boston Impact Initiative, a place-based impact investing fund with a focus on economic justice.[39] The Boston Impact Initiative has a history of actively working with economically challenged areas around Boston, creating community, jobs, and cooperative endeavors, and providing opportunity for economic and financial participation.

I learned about the RSF Social Finance and their work with social entrepreneurs.[40] I invested in Kiva giving microloans to individuals who would not otherwise be able to access capital. I moved some of our retirement funds into CDFIs (Community Development Finan-cial Institution).[41] In my local community, I invested in Homewise, which works to provide affordable housing in New Mexico.[42] I began to offer classes teaching about conscious money and healing our money story. As a couple, we clarified our approach to investing and worked closely with individuals and businesses to support them on their money journey, either to become debt free or to expand their businesses.

We also participated in the gift economy, gifting to people who were doing important community work and needed financial support. I do believe in gifting, that the more I give, the more I receive. Included in those gifts I receive are things that money can't buy like community, beauty, a new insight, a new connection, or new knowledge. I also have the deep satisfaction that the work I do has a positive impact in my community.

Summer is a time of fullness. Everything is growing; there is an urgency. All the berries and peaches ripen at once; there's too much zucchini, too many tomatoes. It's the season of farmers' markets. Our days seem ripe and full. It's also a time to be aware of the challenges of excess. Perhaps there is too much heat or too many weeds or too many bugs. It is time to pause, to look at the ways things are growing in our lives. It's an opportunity to evaluate the things we are doing right in our lives, and it's a time to celebrate the goodness and examine how we are moving and growing.

Summer Ritual: Growth and Gratitude

Honoring Summer: In the northern hemisphere, Summer Solstice is celebrated on or about June 21. In the southern hemisphere, it is celebrated on December 21. It is the longest day and the shortest night of the year. This ritual can also be used to celebrate Summer Solstice. If you like, invite a friend or a group to share this ritual with you.

Preparation: If possible, plan to be outside for this Summer ritual. If you do this in the evening, plan to bring a candle or a flashlight. Bring a small bowl of water. Prepare your space with summer flowers or a bowl of gifts from your garden or a nearby clover patch. Include an item that celebrates the sun: a hat or a yellow gemstone. Bring your money journal and a symbol of your money journey; cash or your credit card will work. Bring a pen and paper to write during the ritual. After the ritual, take this paper and place it on your altar, in your planner, or on your bulletin board as a reminder of your commitment to your money intentions.

Begin: Breathe deeply and bring yourself into the present. Connect with the Earth, giving thanks for this time and space. Sprinkle yourself and your space with water for blessing and cleansing.

Opening Prayer

This is my Mother's world and to my listening ear

All Nature sings, around me rings, the music of the spheres

This is my Mother's world, I rest me in the thought

Of rocks and trees, of skies and seas, Her hands the wonders wrought.

This is my Mother's world, the birds their carols raise

The morning light, the lily white, declare their Maker's praise

This is my Mother's world, She shines in all that's fair

In rustling grass, I hear Her pass, She speaks to me everywhere.[43]

Ritual: Gratitude and Intentions for Growth and Abundance

In your money journal, write out a list of five ways you have grown over the Winter, Spring, and Summer. Write out five things for which you are grateful. Next, write out your Summer money intentions: five or six action steps to keep you on your money path for the next six weeks to six months. Decide on your top priority; make a commitment to take action in the next week. Place your cash or credit card on top of your intentions. Hold your hands over your money and your intentions, blessing them with your energy, knowing they are becoming manifest even as you think your thoughts and hold them in your heart.

Closing Prayer: Welcoming Light

> *We welcome you, Light of Inspiration, Light of Spirit, Light never-ending. We celebrate Light and the opportunity and blessings that money brings to our world. We celebrate the wonder of the light of our minds, bodies, and souls as well as our bank accounts. May they be infused with Your Light. I bless myself, my money, my intentions, and my future with Your light. May all money be used to serve the highest and best unfolding for Earth, humanity, and all sentient beings. In thanksgiving for this Light, this Light of Inspiration, this Light Within and Without, we say thank you, and so it is.*
>
> *Blessed Be.*

End of Ritual

Affirmations

- ❖ I am grateful for my abundance.
- ❖ I feel so courageous about my life and my finances.
- ❖ I love to see the growth and changes in my financial life.

Chapter 9
Work

By and large a good rule for finding out is this: the kind of work God usually calls you to is the kind of work (a) that you need most to do and (b) that the world most needs to have done.... The place God calls you to is the place where your deep gladness and the world's deep hunger meet.[44]

—Frederick Buechner, Educator, Writer, Theologian

Work, Meaning, and Service

Work is central to who we are; it is part of our wholeness, our Divinity. We each have our work, the part of us that expresses our life by the way we spend our time. We work, earn money, give back to the world and, hopefully, are allowed self-expression. Most of us spend a good portion of life working in exchange for monetary compensation. Do you remember your first real job, where someone paid you for your efforts? My first job was babysitting, not very glamorous, but it was good to get paid. I also did housecleaning; I worked at a dry goods store; I made tacos at Tijuana Tacos, and I worked as a hostess at Pancho's Restaurant. I was a meter maid on the undergraduate college campus. I tutored English in Mexico during my extended stay after graduation from college. I worked in hospital administration. I did nonprofit consulting. I taught social work classes. I had a naturopath practice. I was an event planner. Some people have one job their entire life. Daniel studied dentistry and has worked as a dentist his entire life. Brianna worked as an engineer for a large corporation, then decided to go into accounting, all the while doing art and music on the side. My friend Patrice ran a private school for years and then entered the ministry as a Methodist minister. But work is beyond just earning money. It's part of our relationship with wages, compensation, and who we are in the workplace and in the world, and it is also how we manifest our Divinity.

But work is beyond just earning money. It's part of our relationship with wages, compensation, and who we are in the workplace and in the world, and it is also how we manifest our Divinity.

The American Heritage Dictionary defines work as physical or mental effort or activity directed toward the production or accomplishment of something. It also has another fourteen definitions. However, we each have our definition of work.

As we look at our big goal, to create a just, sustainable world, it becomes important how we view work and what kind of work we choose to do. In the famous book, *What Color Is Your Parachute?* the authors suggest an in-depth assessment of your preferences for a working environment, location, what you are able to do, and what you want out of your job.[45] It's a wonderful way to find and explore where your desires and skills match the marketplace. But take a deeper look at how you want to be and show up in the world. What are the considerations about working for an employer who does not support the community or one that uses low-paid foreign labor in lieu of paying American workers, or a company that continues to degrade the environment? Work is such a personal choice.

We can bring joy to our customers, our colleagues, and our company. It can give purpose to our actions. A fifth-grade teacher can influence the future of his students in powerful ways—to become lifelong learners, better writers, and insightful scientists—all by the age of ten. A doctor can change the health and well-being of her patients. A supervisor can support workers to grow and thrive.

Work can be a venue to support others on their personal journey. It's a place to celebrate victories and share failures or to impact others in a positive and caring manner. Work allows for personal growth, and allows us to use our skills, talents, and creativity. Ideally, work would feature and display our best talents.

A recent McKinsey report indicates that people who live their purpose at work are more productive than people who don't; they are also healthier, more resilient, and more likely to stay at the company when employees feel that their purpose is aligned with the *organization's* purpose.[46] For most of us, work is essential, and meaningful work provides us with both income and meaning.[47]

A New Work Template

I've learned that making a living is not the same thing as making a life.
– Maya Angelou

By looking at money through a spiritual lens, work is also a place to bring our spiritual life into focus and service. What is the gift you want to share with the world? What is the purpose to which you want to dedicate your time and attention? What is the call you have to be of service to your community and to the world?

Working with a life coach a few years ago, we spent blessed time talking about work, what work meant to me, how I wanted to work, and my personal perspectives about work. It was a wonderful, eye-opening experience. I realized that my (old) view of work was a template of burden, sadness, and toil. More specifically, when I looked inside and saw my work template, it was an old, wooden, rusted, hand plow. In my mind's eye, the handles were splintered, and it required me to push it down long rows of work. It was hard, burdensome, and never-ending.

When I was a child, my grandfather had a large garden, and he had a hand plow. I remember it being hard work to cultivate the hard-packed dirt of the Arizona mountains. My template of work was one that had no joy or beauty. I needed a new template.

I journaled. I thought about what I wanted to include in my personal work template. What would serve as a daily reminder to me that my work could be beautiful, joyful, and serve me and others? After much discernment and pondering, I decided on flowers as my new work template. I downloaded a bunch of photos of beautiful flower arrangements, and I went to flower shops and took photographs of beautiful arrangements. I found a sweet silk flower arrangement to put on my desk and I bought a beautiful art piece with a variety of flowers, framed in a large gold frame to hang on the wall in my office. Flowers give me so much joy! I delight in the miracle and beauty of flowers by bringing them into my daily work and my life.

With my new template in place, I had a very different attitude toward my work in the world. I saw it as something of beauty, not something burdensome and hard. It also shifted the way I felt about money. I could see the service and the gifts I wanted to share from a much broader, more spacious perspective. What a lovely change for me!

EXERCISE

Work Template

Using your money journal, take as much time as you need to ponder your work template. Go to your quiet space, breathe deeply, and allow yourself to become calm and relaxed. Now think about what work means to you, and find a shape, an image, a color that represents your current work situation, where you are, and how you feel about it right now. It could be a pile of paper, a building, or a kids' set of Legos. What sort of image, picture, or item describes your current pattern? Get acquainted with this and find the details about this that have meaning. Maybe the piles of paper represent money tasks that need to be addressed. Perhaps the building symbolizes structures that need remodeling.

Next, ask yourself how your new work template might look; open your mind's eye. What do you see? How do you feel? What is emerging in this scene that draws your attention? Is there an object or item that you see? Approach this new template, look at it, touch it, and allow it to form with color, texture, space, and depth. Describe it out loud to yourself. Describe its features; what does it look like? Is it big, small, hard, soft, dark, light, something you are familiar with, or something you never considered? Spend some time looking at the details, the edges, the shape, and the mass.

Once you have an idea for a new work template, journal about it in your money journal and find or purchase an object to remind you of your new way of being about work.

Affirmations

- ❖ I feel so blessed to do my work in the world.
- ❖ I am healed and restored as I do my work.
- ❖ I allow money and work to lift and support me.

Chapter 10
Mindful Consumerism

The world has enough for everyone's need, but not enough for everyone's greed.
—Mahatma Gandhi

Mindful or conscious consumerism is a growing trend. It is the practice of buying while considering the social, economic, and environmental impact of your decision. It is an opportunity for each of us to "vote" with our dollars and to decide where we want our time, attention, and money to go. Conscious consumerism is an alert mindset about what we think is important in our lives. This includes clothing, food, transportation, health, and housing—all the areas of our daily lives. By becoming conscious consumers, we help ourselves, our communities, and our environment, and help protect precious natural resources for future generations. Reduce, reuse, recycle: These are the basic tenets of conscious consumerism.

Unconscious Consumerism

We live in a society where we want everything, RIGHT NOW! Even if we can't pay for it, we use credit to meet today's wants, without regard to future impact. We live in a society that tells us that if we don't have the right clothes, toothpaste, medicine, or car, we aren't good enough. We live in a consumer culture built on accumulation and MORE, BIGGER, BETTER as the reigning message in almost every industry, business, company, and social media outlet.

Moreover, we have advertisements inundating us through marketing and social media. Stores, websites, magazines, and companies all vie for our attention and push us to buy things we really don't need or want. This is called unconscious consumerism, and the impulse buy of a chocolate bar at the supermarket is a perfect example.

To live with consciousness, we must learn to live between the extremes of deficiency and excess. It's also a decision between wants and needs. What we want and what we need can be in conflict. We need housing, but how big of a house becomes excessive? We need a phone, but is a brand-new, latest model on the market with all those bells and whistles necessary? Yes, we need clothing, but do we need this year's latest styles? As we think through what is important to us and what is enough, it becomes clearer what is essential and what is excessive.

I totally understand that self-gratification and self-indulgence are part of the mainstream promotions for having more, bigger, and better. Think of the advertisements to entice you to trade in your perfectly fine car for this year's upgrade, or the marketing to entice you to buy unhealthy soft drinks or fast food. Taking time to ponder what we need, what we want, and how we want to be in this consumer world is an important process. It's part of our Summer weeding. Going back to our centering practices, we can take time and take a recess or rest and allow ourselves a perspective of needs and wants. Then our choices come from our internal decisions rather than from the dictates of the outside world.

Changing our patterns of consumption is one way to practice conscious awareness of money and a conscious lifestyle.

List of actions you could take to become a conscious consumer:

- Think before you buy. Decide if you need this item (or do you already have five pairs of black pants hanging in your closet?). Differentiate between necessary purchases and impulse or unnecessary purchases.
- Buy used at second-hand stores or specialty consignment stores. Check online for lightly used items for your home or business.
- Choose reusable items. Coffee cups, drink bottles, straws, and silverware can be reused. Avoid single-use plastics such as water bottles, plastic straws, or plastic silverware.
- Repair broken items rather than purchasing a replacement.
- Purchase Earth-friendly products, made from natural materials. Choose environmentally friendly gifts, baby products, toiletries, and cosmetics.
- Look for items that have minimal packaging. This reduces the need for raw materials and reduces waste and costs. Consider buying in bulk if that makes sense for you and your family.
- Buy fair trade: coffee, food, handicrafts, and specialty items.
- Borrow, rent, or share seldom-used items like tools, large equipment, or camping gear.
- Reduce food waste. Compost your kitchen scraps.
- Consider each piece of clothing an investment. Buy only what you need. Keep it clean and in good repair. Avoid fast fashion, cheaply made clothing, and buying what you don't really need.
- Use energy-efficient housing, cars, and appliances.
- Consider the environment and energy required for your transportation and travel plans.

As a conscious consumer, a powerful place to spend your money is at small businesses, local or otherwise. There are hundreds of thousands of small businesses that now can offer their products, services, and information via the internet. It's an amazing technological phenomenon that now allows anyone with an internet connection to share their story and gift.

For example, Goddess Ink is a small, niche publishing company that publishes books on the Divine Feminine and Goddess studies. It appeals to a specific audience, focusing on very specialized information and products. When you buy from Goddess Ink, you are supporting authors and artists who are working in this area.

Etsy is another example of offering handmade products supporting artists, allowing them to earn a living, sell globally, and create custom products. It's another way to support artisans all over the world. Purchasing items directly from the artist allows communication with the artist. You can order specific pieces for your home or your office while you financially support the artist, and you might even become friends.

Building a sustainable future will require each of us to be a steward of this beautiful planet.

I have a lovely friend who is a bead artist. I love buying earrings from her because I know her, she does beautiful work, and I love buying directly from her, supporting her financially, and appreciating her work. Building a sustainable future will require each of us to be a steward of this beautiful planet.

Live responsibly and sustainably. With conscious attention to the small decisions we make, we begin to see our connectedness to nature, others, and the larger systems at work in our world. This awareness leads to compassion and engagement. With this awareness and aliveness, everything has meaning, and we experience the world as a marvelous place to live, full of miracles and magic. We enjoy Summer's bounty.

Needs vs. Wants

What do we need? What do we really need? What do we really, really need?

Yes, there are fundamental needs for survival: housing, food, clothing, transportation, and the basic means of earning a living. However, there are many more things in life that we *think* we need, that have little to do with survival. We may be influenced by products marketed by mainstream media, such as vehicles, skin care products, insurance, medications, soft drinks, or dog food. We may need clothing, but do we need trendy, fast fashion?

From a recent study by the Ellen MacArthur Foundation: "Because people are buying more new clothes, they are using them less: the average piece of clothing is worn 36% fewer times now than it was fifteen years ago."[48] We may need transportation, but do we need a brand-new, top-of-the-line vehicle that requires a large portion of your paycheck each month? Many of us have trouble distinguishing between our needs and wants.

Needs are life necessities: food, shelter, things necessary for you to do your work, health care, and requirements for your life. Wants are things in your life that you choose because you desire them, but if you didn't have them, you could live without them. Examples might be a gym membership, streaming services, or entertainment. Wants are not bad, they are just not necessary to your survival. They can help you accomplish goals and enjoy life. A phone in our society may be a necessity, but is the latest iPhone a want or a need?

What about our longer-term financial goals, such as savings, retirement funds, and paying off debt? You may consider those as a want since they are not immediate needs. However, consider your relationship with money, and take care of those needs as part of putting your finances in place. This is where conscious consumerism becomes important to make decisions, not just for the bank account, but to create a relationship with money and with your life, a life you design, and to be conscious of your decisions. We also need to make sure we put in the time to nourish and care for our spirit.

This is where conscious consumerism becomes important to make decisions, not just for the bank account, but to create a relationship with money and with your life, a life you design, and to be conscious of your decisions.

What do you *need* to be your best self, to be able to work, share, and connect deeply with others? For Evan, it's making music in his studio, playing mandolin, and writing songs. For Donna, it's creating art, on canvas, on the side of a wall, sketching, and mixing colors. For Hannah, it's digging in her garden; she thrives when she is planting and growing vegetables and herbs. Reggie thrives by being in nature, hiking, watching the hawks, or sitting in the sun. By identifying what we really need to thrive and not being pressured or influenced by external factors, we can create a life that works.

EXERCISE

Conscious Consumption

Identify one area of your life where you can be a more conscious consumer. Take action. For example, support a local artisan, purchase fair trade coffee or chocolate, consider how you can reduce the packaging on what you purchase, or make a commitment to composting. Write in your journal why this is important to your journey to create a just, sustainable world. Share your observations with one other person.

Affirmations

- I have all the Divine guidance and support I need for this journey.
- I have all I need, and I am grateful.
- I am living the most amazing, abundant life I can imagine.

Chapter 11
Community Capital

Some people are so poor that all they have is money.
—Attributed to Patrick Meagher

LaDean was intent on making sure her money made a difference in her local area. For years, she had banked at one of the big national banks. Feeling a need to be more community-focused, she decided to move her money to a local bank. After researching all the banks in her local area, she found a small Black-owned bank that provided money to BIPOC (Black, indigenous, people of color) residents and businesses. She moved her banking to support those efforts and began a new personal relationship with her banker.

Place-based Beingness

One of the diseases or, at the very least, a deep sadness of our times is feeling disconnected. How many of us have felt detached and separate from our family, friends, and neighbors? How familiar are you with the place and space where you live, the plants, the animals, the rivers, the rocks, and the trees? These are all part of our local place and space. Do you know your community, your town, your city, or your district? Do you consider yourself a native, a resident, a citizen, or a visitor, or, perhaps, an outsider?

Building community is a decision and a blessing. We currently live in a community where we share the benefits of a large orchard. We do not own the orchard, but we share in the community upkeep, pruning, and harvesting of the apples, pears, plums, and peaches that are nature's bounty. We share in the delight of connecting with our neighbors and their families who come to take part in the work and the harvest. We also participate in a community garden with about forty other individuals and families. We share seeds, produce, and recipes as well as weeds, mosquitos, and cleanup. It's a gift to be part of this community.

Living locally and connecting to our place and space allows us to connect with others, and ideally, participate in improving our local area. Yes, we acknowledge there are things to upgrade, but it's our association with our locale that provides us with the opportunity to shape, influence, and determine outcomes. Time and attention on our local community can have a big influence.

There are a variety of ways to connect with your local community. Obviously, getting to know your neighbors is a great first step. When new neighbors move in, welcome them with a plate of cookies and let them know you are available. If that doesn't work in your neighborhood, consider planning a block party or sign up on the NextDoor app. Plan a regular visit to the local farmer's market, or start a neighborhood book club. You can attend the local music or dance gatherings. Check with the library and the city about educational programs, cleanup days, and city-sponsored summer festivals. Invite your neighbors to join you on a bike ride, a visit to the botanical garden, or to support your local bank, restaurant, or coffee shop. Summer's abundance invites us to pass the bounty around.

I deeply value our connection to our local community.

When we lived in Las Cruces, we banked with our locally owned bank, and we knew some of the employees. We have a personal relationship with our bank vice president that we have built over the years. I can call her with any questions about our bank accounts. If she doesn't know, she will get back to me. That relationship is valuable to me, and I appreciate that I have a person I can call who knows me. Big national banks have phone contacts but mostly they are faceless customer service representatives who do not know me. There is something precious about having that personal relationship. Since we moved, we have developed a personal relationship at our local credit union in order to support the community and foster a positive relationship while banking locally.

Local focus can mean proximity for purchasing local food or local goods. Buying local beer means a lower carbon footprint. As much as I love wine from Argentina and Spain, I purchase local or domestic options. Local economies, markets, and businesses are more personal. Business owners and residents build relationships and social networks. It is fun to learn about the people selling at the local farmers' market. A trip to pick up vegetables at the local Community Supported Agriculture (CSA) provides a peek at the garden where the vegetables were grown and harvested. There is something sacred and holy about honoring the place where you live.

There is something sacred and holy about honoring the place where you live.

I live in an agricultural area of a large metropolitan area. I feel grateful to live where I live. I love the trees, the sky, the mountains, and the pastures. I also cherish the history, the people, and the interesting characters and activities that populate my community. I want my city and state to thrive and be a wholesome, healthy place for everyone who lives and visits here.

When you look at your local economy as a system, consider its similarities to the human body. We have blood, but we are not blood;

we have bones, but we are not bones. We have local businesses, but we are not only local businesses; we have our local community neighborhoods, but we are not only those neighborhoods; we are a confluence of people, places, and interests. How can we direct our relationships and our money to our community?

Here are some easy ideas for connecting with your local economy: join a local giving circle, shop locally, support local funding initiatives, attend concerts and performances of local artists, support community events.[49]

Local Multiplier Effect

Have you considered the impact of spending your dollar locally?

The local multiplier effect is the result of independent, locally owned businesses which recirculate a greater percentage of revenue than nonlocal businesses or locally owned franchises.

The American Independent Business Alliance states that the local multiplier effect is composed of three elements: direct, indirect, and induced impacts. The direct impact is the spending done by local businesses to operate a business, including pay to employees, spending on inventory, equipment, and other business expenses. The indirect effects are the dollars that recirculate as a result of spending by a local business. For example, a locally owned restaurant, Rosita's Mexican Restaurant, sells local food and pays suppliers, employees, and taxes. The induced multiplier effect is because the owners, workers, and others then spend the money they received as a result of doing business with the restaurant. It means local businesses hire more people locally, and pay more taxes, so the local government can employ more police, pave more roads, and improve the quality of your life.

"On average, 48 percent of each purchase at local independent businesses was recirculated locally, compared to less than 14 percent of purchases at chain stores.

"The Institute for Local Self-Reliance conducted perhaps the simplest study of the local multiplier effect in several small Maine communities. The study examined how much of a dollar spent at a local independent store is re-spent in the local area as payroll, goods/services purchased from area businesses, profits spent locally by owners, and as donations to area charities.

"ISLR's study found that $100 spent at local independents generated $45 of local spending, compared to $14 for a big-box chain."[50] In other words, keeping your money local has big benefits. Local businesses are key to thriving, healthy towns, cities, and municipalities.

They promote social connections, charitable giving, tourism, and self-reliance. Focusing on our local area, we support economic stability, local sustainability, and local philanthropy. We can also welcome tourists to get the local flavor and community offerings. Furthermore, local businesses are resilient, and they can provide support for community problem-solving. Community-friendly financing can support local businesses, provide local decision-making, and hopefully provide a rate of return that is fair, just, and sustainable for everyone involved.

In other words, keeping your money local has big benefits. Local businesses are key to thriving, healthy towns, cities, and municipalities.

Small business is at the heart of American business. According to the Small Business Administration (SBA), in 2019 (latest data) there were 6.1 million employer firms, and businesses with fewer than one-hundred employees accounted for 98.1 percent of those businesses. America is overwhelmingly small businesses, and the bulk of job creation comes from those small businesses.[51]

Dana Koller is the owner of a small brewery in Central New Mexico called Kactus Brewery. Started in an old garage, the brewery now features craft beer, organic local food, and a sweet gathering spot for local residents and beer aficionados alike. By employing local people, connecting with local suppliers, and generously participating in the local economy through business, charitable giving, and events, Kactus Brewery supports the local community in multiple ways. Dana has participated in the community as president of the Rotary Club, and now he's building a local nonprofit organization called UN-17 to promote the United Nations Sustainable Development Goals for small businesses. Here are ways you can support your local business community:

- Get to know your neighbors and participate in neighborhood activities.
- Attend local events at the library, music or dance festivals, and city-sponsored events.
- Volunteer at the local food bank, animal shelter, or community garden.
- Join the local historical society, botanical garden, or museum, and participate in local events.
- Support your local restaurant, coffee shop, candy shop, bakery, bike shop, brewery, bookstore, garden, or herb shop.
- Participate in the local food cooperative or join a local Community Supported Agriculture (CSA) or support the local vendors at your local farmers' market.

Food and Cooperatives

Food Cooperatives have been around since 1844 and began with a group of individuals called the Rochdale Society of Equitable Pioneers.[52] This was mainly a group of weavers who banded together to open a store that would provide food for their families with a small initial investment and the opportunity to benefit by purchasing groceries in bulk. They also provided for a patronage dividend. The group drew up the now famous Rochdale Principles for cooperatives:

- Voluntary and open membership
- Democratic member control
- Member economic participation
- Autonomy and independence
- Education, training, and information
- Cooperation among cooperatives
- Concern for the community

By 1900, there were over 1400 British cooperatives.

There was a resurgence of interest in cooperatives in the late 1960s. Since then, they continue to supply groceries and goods to many communities. I belong to my local food co-op and appreciate the member benefits, the community, the education, and the support given to local farmers. My first venture with a food co-op was in college. There was a two-room building where, once a week, a food truck would deliver wonderful vegetables, fruits, cheeses, beans, and flour. As volunteers, we were assigned to package the products and prepare the items for sale. There were great people bringing in organic and healthy food while building the local community.

Cooperative businesses are member-owned businesses operated for the benefit of their members. Consumers, workers, and community members can all "own" a portion of the business. In the United States, a common cooperative is the natural grocery store. There are other large businesses such as housing co-ops, and electrical or rural co-ops that have member benefits. Being a member of a cooperative allows member benefits such as ownership, decision-making, discounts, and dividend distribution. Check in your local community for a food co-op; it's a wonderful way to make connections in your community.

After participating in the local co-op in southern New Mexico as a member, I finally joined the board of directors, assisted in drafting store policy, looked over financials, and helped to create community events. When I moved to Albuquerque, I participated in a cooperative loan program where local farmers could borrow money for seeds, fertilizer, or support until crops came in. We invested $5000 at a 1 percent return, focusing not on the ROI but rather on the benefit to the community.

What Summer crops do you want to tend?

Community Banking/CDFI, Public Banking, Credit Unions: Where Does Your Money Spend the Night?

Where does your money spend the night? Is it in a small local bank, that gives the majority of its loans to the local community? Is it in a local credit union, which pays dividends to its members? Or is it sitting in a big-name bank, funding fossil fuels, or systematically excluding women and communities of color from financial services? Consider this: "All six of the US banking giants are in the top dirty dozen fossil banks, accounting for a whopping 37 percent of global fossil fuel financing since the Paris Agreement was adopted."[53] Being thoughtful about where you bank, what credit card you use, and where you spend all have an impact.

Let's talk about cash and cash equivalents. Why is this important? First of all, we all need to have our three- to six-month life support fund available to us. Additionally, if we are getting ready to make a big purchase or getting ready to retire, we may be stashing away extra funds for those projects or events. These funds could be working for you and the causes that matter to you. Second, there is an opportunity to put cash into safe and impactful investments. Third, cash investments are usually low risk and low return but there's also a low barrier to entry: You can invest for as little as $25 or $100. This cash could be checking, savings, or money markets, or certificates of deposit. Additionally, if you use credit cards issued by a local bank or an organization you support, the profits and fees are funding loans and services that support your issues. If you use cash in your local exchanges with vendors, you can increase their profit, because they are not paying financial service fees for credit card processing.

Your Banking Relationship

Consider your bank. What is the impact of that decision? "According to the Independent Community Bankers of America, despite the huge number of megabank branches across the country, community banks provide nearly 60 percent of small business loans. In rural areas, the impact of community banks and credit unions is even greater as they provide 80 percent of national agricultural loans."[54] The impact of banking with a community bank is enormous.

Banking is a personal and weighty decision. We have to consider banking and digital services, fees, account protection, balance requirements, location, and convenience. There are a variety of local banks and credit unions, as well as socially responsible online banks.[55] Additionally, there are also a variety of green credit cards.[56] These cards generally focus on rewards and incentives that benefit environmentally friendly businesses and spending. These are a couple of ways you can be involved with your cash and credit card to have an impact in a positive way. How might you begin? Here are some possible local impact actions:

- Pay local vendors in cash, so they are not having to pay the financial/credit card systems 3 percent of their profit.
- Move your banking to a local bank or credit union.

EXERCISE

Banking

1. First, make a list of all the places you might have cash, bank accounts, and savings accounts. Decide what you want to do with those resources to have an impact. (See Chapter 16 for more information about investing.)
2. Find a local bank, credit union, Community Development Financial Institution,[57] or digital bank that serves and benefits your impact area. Bank for Good is an organization working as a coalition of "banks, credit unions, and other financial institutions committed to a fossil-free future, and we wanted to make it easy for you to find them and join the movement."[58]
3. Do your due diligence, and make sure this bank has the types of products, services, community, environmental, social, or governance focus that are important to you.
4. Open an account, order new debit cards, and move your paycheck deposits, savings, and bill pay accounts to your new bank account.
5. Apply for a green credit card and choose an account that supports your interests.
6. Break up with your big bank. Close your account with Big Bank and move your money to a local or socially responsible bank.

Affirmations

- I easily manage my banking, my money, and my assets with Divine guidance.
- I allow grace, ease, and flow as I move my money with intention.
- I am so grateful for my creative approach to life and money.

Part Five

Autumn

A fallen leaf is summer's wave goodbye.
—Anonymous

Autumn is that interesting season of transition, from the heat and action of summer to the quiet and silence of winter. The autumn cycle is about the fullness of life, ripeness, and harvest. The garden is primed to share the abundance and ready itself for moving to the stillness of winter. Harvest begins, the apples have been picked, the grapes are harvested, the fields turn yellow and brown, and we give thanks for the last of fresh morsels from the garden. The leaves turn loose and shower us with beautiful fall color and crunchy, dry foliage to walk in or play in, if we are so inclined. Corn mazes and pumpkin patches dot the rural landscapes.

Harvest is cause for celebration, for Spring's assurance and Summer's growth have come to fruition.

Autumn is also the season of celebrating. We gather our crops, collect the fruit, bring in the bounty, and prepare and store it with care. Knowing what you planted and tended allows for assurance that during the dark time of winter, we have the benefits of our harvest on which to rely.

There are many fall celebrations for harvest time: Thanksgiving in the US, Diwali, the Indian Festival of Lights. Many Native American communities have harvest fiestas; many honor ancestors during the Dia de Los Muertos celebration, and Octoberfest is celebrated in Europe and worldwide.

Autumn also has to do with the inner journey, reflections, and slowing down. We celebrate the Autumnal Equinox in the northern hemisphere and the Vernal Equinox in the southern hemisphere on September 23. It's a time when day and night are equal, and light and dark are balanced. It's a time to look at the balance in our life; yes, there is a swirl of both dark and light, shadow and bright, the black of the night, and the radiance of the sun. It's also a reminder of the transformation from birth and growth back to the season of decay and death.

During this Autumn journey, we will be talking about the harvest of our transition from the *Me, More, Mine* world view to the *Us, We, and the Earth* new paradigm. In Chapter 12, we talk about global well-being and the United Nations Sustainable Development Goals as well as a couple of examples of global efforts to improve our world. In Chapter 13, we dive into examples and ways to promote a sharing, gifting economy. In Chapter 14, we delve into investing in a new, caring, and sustainable economy.

My Autumn Story

I don't consider myself wealthy because of my bank account. I consider myself wealthy because of my relationships, the place where I live, because of the generosity of Mother Nature, and because I am able to live a full, interesting, engaging, and creative life. I consider myself a money steward—that is now my work. Neither Paul nor I came from wealthy families, yet, with his talent for making and saving money and our inclination for frugal living, we have managed to acquire enough financial security to be comfortable and help others on the way.

Currently my husband and I use our retirement funds to invest in our neighbors, our community, small businesses, real estate, and help people out of credit card debt. We have a self-directed individual retirement account (SDIRA).[59] It is one of the many tax-deferred saving options for a retirement account.[60] Instead of investing in Wall Street or in companies I know nothing about, we try to focus on placing our money where it will have an impact. It is not always easy, but it's extremely interesting and the non-financial rewards are much bigger than the comparatively low-interest rates we charge on our loans.

We began twenty years ago when a friend of mine was having financial issues. She was deep in credit card debt and asked if we could assist her to consolidate her debt and reduce her high-interest payments. We were able to consolidate her debt and she made one lower interest payment to us. She made these arrangements with my husband. She was enormously grateful to Paul for his kindness and non-judgment of her circumstances and his patience with her lack of money savvy. She was so appreciative that our loan helped her get back on financial track. Since those dark days, she has thrived. She owns a beautiful condo and stays on track with her business and personal accounts.

Over the last decade, we have made loans to individuals and small businesses, usually in our community. These are person-to-person loans, where we sit together eyeball to eyeball and talk frankly, openly, and honestly about the situation. We have often found that more than money, people often need education and ideas on how to track and manage their money. We have spent many an hour looking over income and expense reports, discussing options, and refining plans of action. In the process, we have consolidated business debt, we have loaned money for school tuition, new roofs, and construction projects. We funded new music studio equipment and the renovation of a dilapidated downtown house into a trendy bar. We have helped save more than one house from foreclosure and helped individuals out of high-interest payday loan misadventures. This work helps our neighbors, keeps our retirement funds in circulation, and gives us a sense of satisfaction that we are doing something positive in the world.

As a couple, Paul and I have had both successes and failures in both spending and investing. The rewards are greatest in the connections and relationships we build with our friends and clients. Our story, our approach, and our process are unique to us.

I will also say not every loan is a success. Of course, we have had our failures. We have made loans that were not paid back. We have loans that need constant attention and many revisions due to changes in circumstances, income, or expenses. We have invested in companies where the technology looked great, but the management team didn't have a good handle on finances, and ultimately the business failed. We invested in companies that didn't survive COVID. We have forgiven loans, for example, when a single mom could no longer make payments on her loan. We have participated in investing in small businesses as equity partners but have found start-up businesses are too risky for us. After a couple of experiences with those small businesses folding, where we lost all our investment, we have mostly focused on lending or providing credit from our retirement account. Personally, another reason for me not to do equity deals is, truthfully, I don't want to leave each of my four grown children a small piece of some small business. These are our retirement funds, and we have decided to be quite conservative with these investments.

As a financial team, Paul and I each have different gifts. Paul has thirty-five years of experience as a CPA; he understands business and financial statements and has worked with hundreds of clients talking about business, finances, and money. He keeps track of the contracts, the bookkeeping, the files, and the financial oversight. I take care of much of the client communication, meetings, and agendas. I've learned to ask clarifying questions. I remember to ask about the person, not just the numbers. I make sure each one is a caring, relationship-based conversation, not just a financial transaction. We work with clients to provide education, guidance, and support, and to resolve debt issues. Each situation is different, and each solution is unique to that person. It's quite interesting, but unfortunately it is not scalable. Nonetheless, it allows me to use my money with impact.

Another decision for using our money in our community is in the form of gifting to people or situations that need support. Julia works with inner-city refugee kids, helping with tutoring, and life skills, and providing a safe, engaging environment for her neighborhood kids. When her work hours were reduced because of the COVID pandemic, we were able to pay half her rent for several months until she found a job that could support her and her work with the kids. We pay the cell phone bill for a single mother, so she has internet access and a phone. These are small ways of helping the world but meaningful to me and those individuals.

Another way that I invest my experience and knowledge about money is by teaching and sharing about our connection between the sacred and finance.

A couple of years ago, a colleague invited me to participate in an online panel discussion at a national finance and investing conference. There were four of us on the panel and we had to write a description of our talk. One of the panel members wrote a description using what I considered to be a financial word puzzle with phrases like "hybrid term sheets" and "liquidity incentives." It didn't make sense to me, and it wasn't how I wanted to present alternative investment options to the public. After rewriting the description into understandable English, I had a big ah-ha moment in which I realized that, one, my input matters, and two, the place that I can really contribute is by bringing in the beautiful, inspiring spiritual aspects not generally found in financial conversations.

My edits of the panel description, which the group approved, included language about "the triple bottom line," "fair for entrepreneurs and investors," and "structures of investment for building community as well as building wealth." This was a big win for me, and clarified for me that it's okay I don't know all the big investment and finance language; I can bring inspiration, creativity, and a people focus into the conversation on how to build a more just, sustainable, thriving Earth!

I remember when I said, "I don't know how to read financial statements. I don't know what assets or liabilities are, or how to do due diligence." It was a mystery to me. Even now, those skills are not my strong point, but I have, with time, become more comfortable with looking at, discussing, and working with financial statements and other elements of the financial world. Another focus for me with money is finding how we can build healthy relationships around money, bringing in caring and compassion rather than just cold, impersonal transactions. What I realize is that I am more comfortable asking questions and grasping the bigger picture, and seeing the impact than when I started on this money journey. I also realize I don't have to know everything.

I work to recall that I am creative, resourceful, and resilient, and I have value just because like you, I am a living, breathing participant in this amazing world. I recognize that I am complete, whole, and empowered by the life force energy that brings everything from a seed to harvest. I value myself, my voice, my opinion, and my observations. I am my own inner authority. I make decisions and choices that support me, my family, and my community, and which, hopefully, extend out to the wider world. I continue to reflect on how to live in this world, and how to use my resources of time, money, and focus to create a just, sustainable world. This is my Autumn harvest.

My goal these days is to be thoughtful and involved in how my money impacts the world. I want to take an active role, think deeply, do my research, have an opinion, and make decisions, not to stifle my voice, or to accept someone else's suggestions or recommendations just because they have credentials I don't have. I want to engage others in conversation about how to use money and the sacred self as a tool to transform the world.

My decisions to participate in groups, investments, and with individuals who foster a sustainable future are important to me. I also want to participate in the gift economy. What I realize is as I gift, I too am gifted by the experience and by the generosity of others who gift their care, knowledge, and bounty to me and my community. I continue to be encouraged by the unselfishness of Susan, who donates time and money to projects in Ghana. I marvel at Keith, who fixes and donates bicycles across the US-Mexico border. I am inspired by Ryan who works with entrepreneurs who are building new green technology or researching an innovative medicine to heal diabetes. I love looking at the larger globe and giving a vision of how to make our world a better place to be and live. Author Charles Eisenstein writes about this larger vision in his book *The More Beautiful World Our Hearts Know Is Possible*, he says, "That we are fundamentally unseparate from each other, from all beings, and from the universe. That every person we encounter and every experience we have mirrors something in ourselves. That humanity is meant to join fully the tribe of all life on Earth, offering our uniquely human gifts toward the well-being and development of the whole." [61] We all have an impact; the question is what kind of impact do you want to have in your world?

In this season of Autumn, in Chapter 12, we will explore conscious capital and global well-being. In Chapter 13, we investigate the sharing economy. Finally, in Chapter 14, we dive into conscious investing. For me, the season of Autumn is a time to reflect on the growth in my spiritual life, as well as how I am choosing to use my money. It's a time of gratitude, of sharing my abundance, and of being thoughtful of how I want to engage with the world.

First, let's celebrate Autumn with a harvest ritual.

Autumn Ritual: Harvest

This may be a ritual to invite others to celebrate with you. Consider inviting your partner or others who have supported your money journey, so they may share in your harvest success.

Preparation: Prepare a space with a harvest candle. Prepare symbols of your journey, your successes, and your blessings. Bring examples that represent your money success and your commitment to this work. For example, it may be the receipt for a money course to help keep you on track, a thank you note from a friend for some assistance you provided, or a copy of your completed estate documents. What do you want to honor as symbols of your money and spirit journey? Bring that with you to this ritual. To celebrate your harvest, bring a treat for yourself: chocolate, a glass of wine, or some treat that you can appreciate at the end of the ceremony. Light the candle.

Lay your items of money success and harvest on the table or altar, along with your treat for the end of the ceremony. Begin with silence and deep, luxurious breaths, feeling the air, checking in with your body, and appreciating the time to be still. Begin when you are ready.

Opening Prayer:

> *Divine Source, I greet you with a grateful heart. I thank you for this time with You. Beloved, your abundant generosity feeds the world. Your abundant caring comforts our hearts. Your abundant wisdom allows the cycle of birthing and dying. Your abundant love provides us with the sweetness of our lives. I give thanks for money as love in action. I release money and give*

thanks allowing this flow in and this flow out, streaming with blessings and serving the highest and best for all. I live fully in this grace and flow of the spirit of good and plenty.

Ritual Reading

Blessed are you, Autumn, chalice of transformation. You lift a cup of death to our lips, and we taste new life. Blessed are you, Autumn, the season of the heart's yearning. You usher us into places of mystery, and, like the leaves, we fall trustingly into eternal, unseen hands. Blessed are you, Autumn, with your flair for drama. You call to the poet in our hearts, "Return to the Earth, become good soil; wait for new seeds." Blessed are you, Autumn, you turn our faces toward the west. Prayerfully reflecting on life's transitory nature, we sense all things moving toward life-giving death. Blessed are you, Autumn, you draw us away from Summer's hot breath. As your air becomes frosty and cool, you lead us to inner reflection. Blessed are you, Autumn, the season of so much bounty. You invite us to imitate your generosity in giving freely from the goodness of our lives, holding nothing back. Blessed are you, Autumn, your harvesting time has come. As we gather your riches into our barns, reveal to us our own inner riches waiting to be harvested. Blessed are you, Autumn, the season of surrender. You teach us the wisdom of letting go as you draw us into new ways of living. Blessed are you, Autumn, the season of unpredictability. You inspire us to be flexible to learn from our shifting moods. Blessed are you, Autumn, feast of thanksgiving. You change our hearts into fountains of gratitude as we receive your gracious gifts.[62]

Harvest Ritual

Hold each of your items of money success, give thanks for the success, and make sure you smile and appreciate your success. Feel and share success in your heart and in your body. If you choose, sing a song of thanksgiving for this harvest and this bounty. Dance a dance of gratitude, celebrating all you have experienced. If you are celebrating with others, share the successes of your journey.

Closing Harvest Prayer

For life, strength, energy, vitality, and the times those gifts seem far away; we give thanks.

For this journey of spirit and money; we give thanks.

For the magnificent, dazzling, and abundant fruits of our planet Earth; we give thanks.

For the powerful blessings of relationship, connection, and love; we give thanks.

For the remarkable potency, skill, and power of our work; we give thanks.

For wonder, creativity, inspiration, and beauty; we give thanks.

For those we know and love and for those we don't know, who need our love; we give thanks.

For our own Divine Nature, Our Sacred Self; we give thanks, we give thanks, we give thanks.

End of ritual. Enjoy your treat!

Affirmations

- ❖ I am free to be my best, fullest, and most authentic self as I walk in the world.
- ❖ I am so much more than the value of my money. I am a precious gift to the world.
- ❖ I am grateful for the blessings, sharing, and caring available to me.

Chapter 12
Conscious Capital

If globalization seeks to bring all of us together but to do so respecting each person, each individual person's peculiarity, that globalization is good and makes us good and grow and leads to peace.
—Pope Francis

Global Well-being

Business can be a force for good in the world. The idea of the triple bottom line (TBL), of considering people, the planet, as well as profit, has been used for many years. It's a wonderful language to consider something other than profit as the main motivation for business. As we consider both the global community and our personal community, it's good to know there are organizations and efforts being made to connect consciousness and capital.

"The term conscious capitalism refers to a socially responsible economic and political philosophy. The premise behind conscious capitalism is that businesses should operate ethically while they pursue profits. This means they should consider serving all involved stakeholders, including their employees, humanity, and the environment—not just their management teams and shareholders. The idea of conscious capital was created by Whole Foods co-founder John Mackey and marketing professor Raj Sisodia."[63]

Conscious Capitalism as an organization states: "We believe that business is good because it creates value, it is ethical because it is based on voluntary exchange, it is noble because it can elevate our existence, and it is heroic because it lifts people out of poverty and creates prosperity. Conscious businesses endeavor to create financial, intellectual, social, cultural, emotional, spiritual, physical, and ecological wealth for all their stakeholders. Conscious businesses will help evolve our world so that billions of people can flourish, leading lives infused with passion, purpose, love, and creativity; a world of freedom, harmony, prosperity, and compassion."[64]

Using four tenets, Conscious Capitalism first suggests that businesses have a higher purpose; that is, business should exist for reasons beyond solely making a profit. Second, there should be a stakeholder orientation, which is to care for everyone involved: employees, customers, suppliers, investors, and society. Third, conscious leaders should be both good stewards and seek creative solutions. The final tenet of Conscious Capitalism is conscious culture, allowing "trust, accountability, transparency, integrity, loyalty, egalitarianism, fairness, personal growth, and love and care."[65]

The Seventeen United Nations Sustainable Development Goals: A Worldwide Agenda for Good

I have a fascination with the United Nations Sustainable Development Goals (UNSDGs). I find it amazing that in 2015, the 193 United Nations member countries agreed to a document that focused on the global future, with goals to achieve that vision. The UNSDGs, also called the 2030 Agenda, is a declaration to eradicate poverty and hunger, protect the planet from degradation, foster peace, prosperity, and partnerships, and improve the lives of people around the planet.

It's a huge agenda, and a wonderful starting point to coalesce efforts toward a just, sustainable world. Wouldn't it be wonderful if our Autumn abundance and harvest could fulfill these goals?

The UNSDGs, also called the 2030 Agenda, is a declaration to eradicate poverty and hunger, protect the planet from degradation, foster peace, prosperity, and partnerships, and improve the lives of people around the planet.

The 2030 Agenda contains seventeen goals which were developed for addressing the world's most pressing issues. It may seem that these goals are unattainable or have nothing to do with your daily life. My view is that everything we do has an impact, so let's make it a positive one. The un.org website has a wonderful pdf which can be downloaded called "The Lazy Person's Guide to Saving the World."[66] This document gives suggestions for things to do from your couch, from your home, things you can do in your neighborhood, and things to do at work.

The seventeen goals are as follows:

- Goal 1: End poverty in all its forms
- Goal 2: Zero Hunger
- Goal 3: Health
- Goal 4: Education
- Goal 5: Gender equality and women's empowerment
- Goal 6: Water and Sanitation
- Goal 7: Energy
- Goal 8: Economic Growth
- Goal 9: Infrastructure, industrialization
- Goal 10: Inequality
- Goal 11: Cities
- Goal 12: Sustainable consumption and production
- Goal 13: Climate Action
- Goal 14: Oceans
- Goal 15: Biodiversity, forests, desertification
- Goal 16: Peace, justice, and strong institutions
- Goal 17: Partnerships[67]

The reason for considering these important components of life on Earth is that first, these goals are achievable—challenging, yes, but achievable. However, with climate change, a worldwide pandemic, increasing economic inequality, and the human threat to the natural world and resources, progress on the goals has been slow. Unfortunately, during the recent COVID-19 pandemic, progress in some areas has been reversed, which is all the more reason to focus on these goals.

According to a report by the World Bank, "Progress toward the SDGs has been uneven. In some of the indicators tracked as part of the SDG framework, there has been clear progress (World Bank 2018a). The number of people living in extreme poverty (i.e., below $1.90 a day) fell by more than one billion between 1990 and 2015 (SDG 1). Globally, more than ninety-five million fewer children were stunted in 2016 than in 1990 (SDG 2). Life expectancy at birth, an important measure of good health and well-being (SDG 3), rose from 65.4 years in 1990 to 72.2 years in 2017. Access to electricity reached 89 percent of the world's population in 2017, up from 83 percent in 2010 (SDG 7; IEA et al. 2019). Yet progress has also been insufficient to meet the 2030 targets in some areas. There are still about one billion people, mostly in rural areas, without electricity. Worldwide, more than half of children do not meet minimum proficiency standards in reading and mathematics (United Nations 2018). As of 2015, 2.3 billion people still did not have access to even basic sanitation services. Recent data indicate that climate change has contributed to a rise in the number of undernourished people (United Nations 2018). Developing strategies to accelerate progress in these areas requires an understanding of the costs connected with meeting the goals."[68]

> The reason for considering these important components of life on Earth is that first, these goals are achievable—challenging, yes, but achievable.

The cost to make significant improvements in the UNSDGs would require investment by countries, public institutions, private businesses, and individuals. According to the United Nations Global Compact, between five to seven trillion dollars would be needed annually to fund the necessary infrastructure to meet the UNSDGs.[69]

Yes, that sounds like a lot of money. However, what if we in the developed countries could see ourselves as global citizens and begin targeting money to eliminate poverty, protect our planet, and foster peace in our world? Do you feel what that might mean to you, to me, to our children and grandchildren, and to future generations?

Examples of Global Good

There are many examples of global good. I invite you to look for your own sources of inspiration in the areas of your interests. One example that inspires me is Angels of Impact. Founded by CEO Laina Greene, Angels of Impact helps women-led micro-enterprises, by providing capital, expertise, volunteer support, and a powerful commitment to a healthy people and planet. "Angels of Impact was started in 2016 by a group of conscious entrepreneurs who believed that we can end poverty sustainably by investing in women led community based sustainable enterprises. We work across Asia Pacific with our presence in Singapore, US and New Zealand. We fund, build capacity and offer a community of learning and support for women leaders working to restore people and the planet."[70]

Born in India, raised in Singapore, and a daughter of immigrant parents, Laina was raised in a family where money was scarce and resources few. After converting to the Baha'i faith, she opened her spiritual world to Oneness, where each person is part of the human family. When each person in the family does well, the whole family benefits. Furthermore, as Laina points out, we need to make decisions with our money, so each person can flourish. To have some people wealthy, and others poor, is contrary to Baha'i teachings. Inspired by microfinance expert Muhammad Yunus's book *Creating a World Without Poverty,* she made a decision to help women, using micro-finance as a model.

Angels of Impact identifies women entrepreneurs, matches them with volunteer support, and supports them with capital raised from individuals who want to support women with low-interest loans. One of Laina's favorite stories is about a mother in a village where the silk industry had been lost to imports and imitation fabrics. One mother saved money to send her daughter off to get an education in the big city. The daughter came back home and started a micro-enterprise of silk weaving. Because of her education and skills, she was able to find markets for the fabric and now the community is engaging in other silk and handmade products from this small town, once decimated by the loss of handcrafted silk production.

Another inspiration in my life is the weekly newsletter from Future Crunch.[71] Founded in 2014, Future Crunch gives a global overview of positive news, and, each month, finds a new, interesting, and impactful charity to support from its subscription funds. It's a powerful, digitally driven, and impressive way to influence the world in a positive way.

EXERCISE

Find a Community or Global Financial Effort You Admire

Take thirty minutes to think about, research, and support in a small way a community or global initiative that supports a changing economic framework. Some ideas might be:

- *The Sharing Economy*
- *The Circular Economy*
- *Corporate Citizenship*
- *Regenerative Agriculture*
- *Environmental Restoration*
- *Financial Equity and Inclusion*

When you find an organization or business that speaks to your interests, sign up for their newsletter, send them a donation, like them on social media, or send their recent blog to a friend for more discussion on the topic.

What did you learn? What inspired you? What action did you take? Note those ideas in your money journal.

Affirmations

- ❖ My money and I create joy and beauty in the world.
- ❖ Using my money and my wealth is an act of thanksgiving and loving service.
- ❖ I am grateful for the opportunity to create a just, sustainable world.

Chapter 13
A Sharing, Gifting, Generous Economy

No one ever became poor by giving.
—Anne Frank

We lived down the road from our friend and farmer Olin, who each week harvested from his large garden for the local farmers' market. Every Friday we would put on grubby clothes, our hats, and gloves, and set out to harvest the week's bounty of lettuce, chard, spinach, beets, peas, cucumbers, squash, and tomatoes. There were delicate bouquets of different lettuce, bundles of radishes to be washed, and boxes of tomatoes to be harvested. We would work in the garden and take home a week's worth of fresh vegetables, plus we were able to spend time outside, with friends, helping with vegetable preparation for the weekly farmers' market. It was a win-win situation for us, our friend, and the community farmers' market.

To me, sharing and gifting are fundamental to who I am as a person, as a member of my community, and as a global citizen. I want to share. I want to extend my offerings of time, expertise, resources, and kindness to those I know, as well as those who live across the globe but need support I can give, financially or otherwise. I want to be a resource. This is how I choose to spread my Autumn abundance.

For example, recently I helped Davin create slides to present his business to a possible investor. We helped Sabina pay for food and lodging as she moved closer to her daughter. I helped Hannah figure out her next steps for securing space for her nonprofit organization. This is part of my life, sharing my gifts and resources; it's part of being a steward of these resources that I have. I also have the wonderful opportunity to receive from others' generosity; for example, I've received apples and pears from a local orchard, a gift of two days at my friend's sweet apartment for a little retreat, and a generous gift of gently used jewelry from my friend Amber. I also realize I must take good care of myself, providing myself with self-care, downtime, and caregiving that I am willing to do for others. It's an intentional plan that gives me time, good food, rest, and recreation. It allows me to develop meaningful relationships. When I do self-care, I can then be available to others, to share and support people and causes that matter to me. That is what the sharing and gifting economy means to me.

Where might you be able to contribute in a non-financial way to your circle, community, or work?

Gifting or Other Mediums of Exchange

Life is a gift. We are given this gift at our birth. The amazing abundance of air, color, sound, taste, and texture is a marvelous mix of magic and sacredness that is easily forgotten in the daily grind of life. Remember, with gratitude and appreciation, the wonder and miracle of nature, plants, stars, and human love. It's a marvel! The powerful thought to recall about gifts and gifting is that YOU are a gift. You—yes, you—are a gift to the world.

Powerfully created to manifest your best self, you have skills, talents, flaws, and challenges in one beautiful package called YOU.

We intuitively know we are each a gift and that gifts are sacred. You are unique, distinctive, and unparalleled in every way. Yes, you and I have shortcomings and imperfections; it's part of being human. No, we can't do everything, but we can gift of ourselves to others. Being generous is a gift, being kind is a gift, and being present to a friend or family member is a gift.

The powerful thought to recall about gifts and gifting is that YOU are a gift. You—yes, you—are a gift to the world.

Greta and Rick hand out coats and blankets for the homeless. Sally gifts reflexology treatments to tired feet. Oliver gifts his time and energy to our community garden. Hard Road, a local bluegrass trio, gifts their musical talents to the local public radio station as an annual fundraiser.

The focus is not on profit or accumulation but on relationships, giving and receiving, connectedness, and generosity. "The obligations and commitments that arise from gifts and their expected return is the glue that holds society together."[72] It's the understanding that we are dependent on each other. Giving and gifting are also about supporting each other, building a sense of community, and cultivating connections. Bartering, sharing, sponsoring, and donating are ways we can each contribute to our community.

Gifting and exchange can be seen as the bonds that hold our world together. It's seeing with pride the value of sharing and contributing to the community. It's not about the value of our possessions or our bank accounts, but about what you GIVE rather than what you HAVE. In a gift economy, such as the potlatches of the Pacific Northwest people, or other native tribes, status is based on how much you give, not what you own.

What if we could begin to honor and value the sharing and caring that comes with a gifting economy?

Bartering is a trade or exchange of goods without the exchange of money in the transaction. Barter trade is common in societies without a big cash economy. Barter is typically an exchange of goods or services to a person who is willing to trade one item or service for another. For example, Heidi, who owns a motorcycle, wants to trade it for her neighbor Jose's boat. Elena, a yoga instructor, needs monthly bookkeeping support and is happy to exchange yoga classes with her accountant Tyrone. Cynthia is taking voice lessons from Kenneth, a jazz musician, and offering her marketing help. There are more sophisticated means of barter, for example, babysitting co-ops, where moms can get six hours of babysitting a month, while providing other moms babysitting, at no cost. There are bartering banks where you can trade an hour of your expertise or service for a service you need. Check your local area or arrange with a friend to exchange what you have for what you need.

Sharing is a relationship builder, a way to connect with others, and a means of giving back to and helping others. We all share. We share our freshly baked cookies with our kids, we share the produce from our garden, and we share our knowledge with our friends, clients, and colleagues. Sharing can become a focus and way of life as well. There are now platforms for couch surfing, where you can share your couch or extra mattress with people from all over the world. There are opportunities to share books as in Little Free Libraries,[73] a global book sharing site. There are opportunities to give away items on marketplace apps like Nextdoor, Facebook, or Craigslist, by listing them as free.

My friend Laurie listed a mattress as free on Craigslist and the daughter of an old friend who had just moved to the community came by to pick it up. It was a delightful reunion for both. In the tech arena, there is open-source software, providing access to a variety of software options that have been developed to provide digital solutions to individuals and businesses.

Sharing, collaboration, cooperation, and reciprocity are all means to a kinder, thriving society.

Microfinance

Microfinance or microcredit is a means of providing small amounts of capital to entrepreneurs or individuals who usually do not have access to financial institutions, or who live in developing countries without access to traditional banking. Pioneered and popularized by Nobel Prize winner Muhammad Yunus, microfinance includes microcredit, micro-insurance, and micro-savings.[74] There are a variety of online opportunities to assist people around the world with a loan. The benefit of providing a loan is that once it is repaid, the money can be loaned again. Often the return on these loans is at zero percent (the loan interest paid by the loan recipient is usually used to support the sponsoring organization). The global microfinance market continues to grow. A recently released report suggests the global market to reach 488 billion by 2030.[75] This is a growing sector for impacting poverty and providing capital in rural or developing areas. Keep in mind, this may be a zero-percent loan, but it is providing valuable support to an entrepreneur who may not otherwise have access to capital.

For example, at Kiva.com, for as little as $25, you can provide a loan for agriculture, small business, energy, housing, education, or medical care. Kiva operates in more than eighty countries and has disbursed more than $1.6 billion in loans.[76] Kiva is only one of many options out there to provide microcredit loans. Grameen Foundation, founded in Bangladesh in 1983, is one of the oldest and most well-known organizations providing micro-banking and non-collateralized loans to alleviate poverty.[77]

Financial Sponsor or Support

Here are recent examples of sponsoring or financial support: When Adelina's husband went to jail, a good friend sent her $100 a month, a huge godsend for her and her then four-year-old son. When Greg was using his expertise and resources to plan and facilitate community conversations, we sent him $600 a month while he looked for a way to support himself and get his nonprofit set up. Donating monthly to a community project to reduce homelessness, providing office space for a start-up business, or paying for car insurance for your cousin who is a single mom might be options to consider. Another way to support individuals is through platforms like Patreon,[78] GoFundMe,[79] or Indiegogo,[80] which provide monthly subscription-based membership, with options for differing levels of support.

Friendship

Friendships are so important to our spiritual and our financial well-being. There are numerous studies showing the benefits of having close friends.[81] Friends allow us to feel understood and appreciated and give us a sense of belonging. Friends help with challenges, provide emotional support, and like us even when we don't like ourselves. Friends share laughter, tears, joys, and sorrows. Despite all the benefits, friendships are often left untended. Making and keeping friends in our consumer society can be a challenge, but the rewards are worth it. As part of your spiritual well-being, consider how you might be a better friend. What are the things you can do to cultivate and nurture your friendships? Consider sending a card, just to say hello to someone far away. Invite someone to coffee whom you would like to get to know better. Reach out to an elder or offer to help a friend with a big task. It's never too late to make a new friend, reconnect with an old friend, or become a better friend by reaching out, being a good listener, or being thoughtful or kind.

Philanthropy

People are generous. According to Giving USA 2021: The Annual Report on Philanthropy for the Year 2020, individuals, bequests, foundations, and corporations gave an estimated $471.44 billion to US charities in 2020.[82] In 2022, 63.9 percent of giving came from individual gifts.[83] Charitable donations are an important sector of our United States economy. We can all give to improve our community.

An interesting treatise by social scientist Arthur C. Brooks, *Why Giving Matters,* states that people who give, volunteer, or even give blood are happier than those who don't. He says, "Acts of charity—giving money, serving others, even donating blood—create a remarkable return, lifting us spiritually and financially." [84] There's even evidence that giving increases your wealth. Families that give more, make more, according to Brooks. Why should you give? Because you will feel better about yourself, because it helps others, and because you will be grateful for the opportunity to help others.

Why should you give? Because you will feel better about yourself, because it helps others, and because you will be grateful for the opportunity to help others.

No, philanthropy will not save the world. It does not fix the structural inequalities of society. At its most basic level, it serves to target money for immediate needs, like donating after Hurricane Katrina in 2005 or supporting bushfire fighting efforts in Australia in 2019.

We are generous in an emergency. There is evidence that people of wealth are giving generously to causes about which they care. There is a movement in the philanthropic world to utilize their investment funds to support socially responsible investing; for example, big funds like the W. K. Kellogg Foundation are working to invest in children, education, and communities with their investments. However, philanthropy will not restructure racism or gender inequality. It cannot solve the climate crisis; it cannot reform global economic inequalities. Those tasks will happen with the collaborative efforts of the private, public, government, and business sectors.

At a personal level, we each need to find the causes, charities, and nonprofit organizations we most want to support, that are doing work that impacts and influences the kind of world in which we want to live. There are so many places to donate and support: the arts, education, health, and the environment. There are animal charities, peace efforts, human rights, and racial justice. There are local, statewide, national, and international charities.

As in all manner of money business, do your research, and make sure the charity is real and not a scam.[85] Charities take money or property depending on the situation.

Here is a list of types of donations that you might consider:

1. Monetary donations—Cash is the simplest form of charitable giving. To claim a tax deduction for your gift, you must have a record or receipt of the contribution.
2. Goods and personal property—Some charities accept donations such as household items, clothing, appliances, or vehicles.
3. Other property—These can include stocks, real estate, art, jewelry, and patents.
4. Leave a bequest in your will or trust to your favorite non-profit organizations. You can decide to leave money or items or both. Put your intentions in writing and let your estate executor know about your gifts.

There are other ways to donate using donor advised funds or charitable trusts. For these types of donations, I suggest speaking with your financial adviser.

A Sharing Economy

There are so many terms out in the world for the sharing economy. Some call it the exchange economy, the collaborative economy, the community-based economy, the peer economy, or the gig economy. I like to consider the sharing economy as a focus on the collective good. It's an economy that is based on relationships and an exchange of tangible or intangible goods.

Technology has allowed the development of many opportunities to participate in the sharing economy. The most often cited examples are house sharing with businesses like Airbnb and Vacation Rental by Owner (VRBO). There are ride sharing options you can use—apps like Uber or Lyft or share a vehicle on Zipcar or Turo. Coworking space is on the rise, where it's possible to share rent, utilities, storage, and office supplies with other professionals. Many cities feature one or more coworking spaces. There are internet sales of the sharing economy, for example, eBay, Craigslist, Facebook Marketplace, and Amazon now allow individuals to sell both new and used goods. This focus is on the internet or platform-facilitated exchanges. Ratings become very important as the trust factor is built on the internet, not on a person-to-person connection. It's a valuable and useful model for exchange but does not always factor in the person, the situation, or the options that might otherwise be available with communication and relationship built into the equation. Other options for participation might be crowdfunding, gifting, financial sponsorship, or philanthropy. What appeals to you?

EXERCISE

Finding Your Comfort in the Sharing Economy

Consider doing one of the following suggestions and write about your experience in your journal.

- Gift one hour a week to an individual or an organization, sharing your time and talent.
- Set up a barter exchange with a friend. For example, you can help with website design, and she can teach you piano.

- Find a microfinance organization that is working in an area of interest to you and invest a small amount in helping someone who needs financial support.
- Support an individual who is struggling with daycare expenses or needing gas money. You can help by paying for a phone, gas, or electric bill. Another idea is to provide a monthly stipend for support. Set a time limit on your gift. We have found six months of support can be very helpful.
- Find a nonprofit organization that is doing good work and donate, volunteer, or leave a bequest in your estate plan.

Affirmations

- ❖ I am grateful to support my community by my gifting, sharing, and participating.
- ❖ I am so pleased to contribute to a just, kind world with my money.
- ❖ I am a global citizen and make responsible money decisions.

Chapter 14
Investing with Impact

What you do makes a difference, and you have to decide what kind of difference you want to make.
—Jane Goodall

Introduction to Investing

If you want to invest in a better world, you can. We all want to make a difference; we all want to have an impact. We want our actions to matter to those we love and to the world; it's part of being human. Conscious investing is about choices, not solely about risk, return, and profit. It's an opportunity to consider people and the planet, not just the gain on an investment. It's about considering the long-term impact of our decisions. It's about allowing the conversation about what it means to have wealth so that the world benefits from our choices. Remember, if you do well, I do well.

After Cecilia's mother died, she called her mother's financial adviser to discuss moving those assets to a socially responsible portfolio. The young enthusiastic financial adviser told her, "Oh no, we could never do that, we are here to make you money." This young man was incorrectly assuming that the only thing that mattered to Cecilia was an economic return. But truthfully, that kind of thinking fuels the capitalistic system, with little regard for the consequences.

As I set out on my own journey into investing, I had to continually go back to my life goals and my spiritual center to ask how I wanted to show up in the world of investing. I still have things to learn, actions to take, and things I don't understand. I'm staying with it because I think it's important to use my money impactfully. It feels a bit like earning a degree in money and spirituality, and the coursework seems to be continuous. It's also been rewarding to feel more in control of my finances, and I'm better able to talk about and work with others on money, finances, and spirituality.

Like other areas of my life, I admit I am a bit of a renegade. When my boys were young, I homeschooled them. I worked on behalf of women priests and left organized religion. I am a certified homeopath, I studied naturopathy, and I use food and nutrition as my basis for staying healthy. I only rarely interact with the medical establishment. Why should it be any different with regard to investing?

I don't think Wall Street, the stock market, or the economic power centers of the world have my best interests, those of my community, or consideration of the Earth in mind as they do their business. I propose we consider thinking about investing in an ecological, social, regenerative, and caring way.

Why Invest and the Trillion Dollar Wealth Transfer

Why should you invest? Perhaps investing feels like it is something other people do, that wealthy people do. Perhaps you have a 401K with your company, but you haven't even looked at what is included in your account.

Investing can feel like a black box: a formidable task, too big to conquer. However, consider that in the next twenty-five years, there will be a $68-$84 TRILLION (not million, not billion) dollar wealth transfer. That is a trillion with twelve zeros ($84,000,000,000,000)! This money will move from the baby boomers (born 1946-1964) to

Gen X (born 1965-1980) and the millennials (born 1981-1996).[86] As the baby boomers age, their wealth and assets are being transferred to their children and grandchildren. A portion of that money will move from the wealthy and the super-wealthy to their heirs. However, there are ordinary people, like you and me, who will also be beneficiaries of this wealth transfer.

I think it behooves us to ask ourselves this question: How will we individually and collectively decide to use this money? Can we stand back and look at the possibilities of living as global citizens? Can we consider ourselves as tenants and stewards of our beautiful Mother Earth, and as relatives of other living creatures? Can we honor with our spirit and with our dollars, and focus on the care and restoration of Earth and water? Can we imagine viewing this capital as an opportunity to expand our impact, and focus on the new paradigm, looking at the broader perspective of inclusion, justice, and a healthy planet? How will we choose what to replant from this Autumn harvest?

Can we imagine viewing this capital as an opportunity to expand our impact, and focus on the new paradigm, looking at the broader perspective of inclusion, justice, and a healthy planet?

I know the financial world of investing is enormous. It can be complicated and discouraging, especially if you are just beginning. There are so many considerations, financial services, financial managers, risk, return, asset classes, cash, stocks, bonds, real estate, and commodities. Add to that the world of digital currencies and cryptocurrency; it can be daunting.

The time it takes to keep up with the market, investment, financial statements, and accounts can be challenging. It can also be interesting, exhilarating, and gratifying to know you are using your money in alignment with your values. You can invest in ways that support the

Earth and are regenerative and sustainable. This is another opportunity to create a sacred relationship with the investment world. In the investing world, it's called impact investing.

Basic Investing and Definitions

If this is your first encounter with investing and using your investments to have a positive impact on the world, perhaps learning a bit more about investments is in order. There are many online options as you consider your next steps. One excellent course focused on women is called Invest for Better.[87] Invest for Better offers a six-month values-aligned investing education program. It's a learning circle, led by trained circle leaders with a robust curriculum and lots of additional information. Another option is to find an online course on one of the programs like Udemy,[88] Corsera,[89] or LinkedIn Learning,[90] or do an internet search for a course that would suit your needs and purposes. Finally, if you are already invested with a bank, investment company, or retirement plan company, they may have educational courses available to you.

In addition to courses, there are great online money journals and podcasts. I will only mention one, The Green Money Journal,[91] founded in 1992 by Cliff Feigenbaum. It is a premier online information hub, packed full of information, videos, an online calendar of events, and focused topics related to money, economics, investing, and sustainability.

This section of the book assumes that you are at a stage in your life where you have some financial stability and have the basics of income and expenses in order. Usually, this is defined as:

- Your income exceeds your expenses on an ongoing basis.
- You have manageable debt, meaning no high interest debt, and you can afford your monthly debt repayments.

- You have three to six months of cash reserves or liquid assets to fund emergency or unexpected expenses.[92]

If you are not there, it's fine. There is no reason for worry, guilt, or shame. Each of us walks our money path at a different pace.

Let's define the word *investing*. This is from Investopedia: "Investing, broadly, is putting money to work for a period of time in some sort of project or undertaking in order to generate positive returns (i.e., profits that exceed the amount of the initial investment). It is the act of allocating resources, usually capital (i.e., money), with the expectation of generating an income, profit, or gains."[93]

That definition does not focus on the positive social benefits that come from investing in a just, kind, sustainable world. This time and focus on your money and finances is a chance for you to look at money through a new lens and a new mindset, from *Me, More, Mine* to *Us, We, and the Earth.* We are the designers of our life; why not design our money and our investments? Let's do investment by design, by *your* design.

The most important place to invest is in yourself. Remember, taking care of your business, and investing in your own personal needs and upgrades are first on the list. Radical self-care and continuing to heal your money story or releasing old patterns that no longer serve you are important steps to creating the future you desire. It's something we all know: "Put on your own oxygen mask first." It's also the easiest part of life to forget. We all have multiple claims on our time, resources, and energy. I recommend doing meditation, prayer, ritual, or ceremony as you move into this area of your life and money. It brings together the financial as well as the inner self to work together to employ your inner wisdom and your dollars.

Reflecting on our investments is a process of thinking and considering the importance of using our money wisely. It answers the questions of why, how, and where to choose to invest money, time, energy, and effort.

Investing goes far beyond the stock market or your 401K. It is investing in the world you want to create. It's about focusing your money on people, places, and things that matter to you. Remember your intentions? Remember your vision of the world you want to create and leave as your Autumn legacy? These are the focus points for investing, because once you are clear on your objectives, then you can look for investments that will support those target areas.

I recommend starting by getting familiar with your current financial portfolio. (See exercise in Chapter 14: Assembling Your Current Financial Portfolio.) Then review where you want to begin to commit your investment funds. You may want to commit a percentage of available funds, or a designated amount to reallocate to specific areas, for example, climate change, renewable energy, or regenerative agriculture. You can look at divesting from specific companies that are involved with fossil fuels, weapons, or companies with poor labor practices. If you choose to invest in specific funds, you can use independent online resources like Morningstar[94] to research company ratings.[95] An online search for the "best socially responsible investments" can give you a starting point for articles or opinions on funds in which you may want to invest.

Also, educating yourself about some of the common terms can be useful. There is so much information online that it can seem overwhelming as investment firms and financial planning services advertise for new clients. My advice is to read about or watch videos to become more familiar with the terms. This chapter is only a small introduction to using your investment dollars for good.

There are various places for you to invest; these are known as asset classes. The most common asset classes are as follows:

- Cash and Cash Alternatives—This asset class includes your savings, checking accounts, cash equivalents such as CDs (certificates of deposit), money market mutual funds, or other funds where you deposit your money, for example, a Community Development Financial Institution (CDFI).
- Fixed Income—Fixed income or bonds are debt instruments where an organization, company, municipality, or government raises money by asking the public for money, with the lender or bondholder to be paid back with interest at the maturity date when the bond is due. This type of investment is a loan. There are a variety of bonds such as treasuries, government agency bonds, municipal bonds, corporate bonds, and impact notes.
- Public Equities—These are stocks sold to shareholders who own a piece of the company. These are sold on stock exchanges such as the New York Stock Exchange (NYSE). There are options for investing by picking individual stocks or investing in funds such as mutual funds, index funds, and exchange-traded funds (ETFs). Yes, there are funds that focus on social impact, and funds that target gender, climate, the environment, and social justice.
- Private or Alternative Investments—These are personally determined investments, unique to your circumstance. The terms of the investment, financial return, and impact are based on individual situations. These investments can be private debt, private equity, angel investing, venture capital, crowdfunding, or real estate.
- Debt, Equity, or Revenue Share Investments
    - A debt investment means you as the investor lend capital and the business will typically repay the loan with an agreed-upon interest and loan term.

   - Equity investments mean the investor buys a portion of a business and the investor shares in the earnings or losses of the business.
   - Revenue sharing allows for the business owner to retain ownership, and it allows for the investor to share in the profits (or losses). For example, a start-up business could have access to capital without debt repayment requirements until the business is successful.

- Risk and Return—The informal rule is, "The higher the risk, the higher the return."[96] All investing involves the possibility or risk of loss. How much risk you are willing to take depends on your risk tolerance and the potential for return on your investment. Each investment has a risk/return trade-off. Risk and return is a very personal matter. Also, depending on the goals for your portfolio—for example, growth versus capital preservation—your tolerance for risk will be different. There are a variety of investment courses that delve deeply into the risk and return relationship.
- Due Diligence What is due diligence and why is it important? Due diligence is the process of researching and gathering information required to make a well-informed and educated decision about investing in a person, fund, start-up enterprise, or business. Due diligence is about asking questions, meeting the team, reading all the associated documents, and making sure you are comfortable with moving forward on the investment. Please keep in mind, due diligence for your investment may be different from mine. However, making sure to ask all your questions and having a level of confidence with the investment is important. The following list is a summary of the information you would need to evaluate a basic investment.

Due Diligence Topics to Research:

- The organization and management team
- Customers, sales, and marketing
- Strategic partners and shareholders
- Product development and intellectual property
- Liabilities
- Financials

- Investment Policy Statement (IPS) —An investment policy statement is a document you create to guide your investment decisions. It can be simple or complex, depending on your goal. Often this will be a document that defines your goals, expectations, time horizons, risk tolerance, and special instructions. It often begins with a description of your assets, liabilities, and net worth. This IPS will take into consideration your retirement situation and retirement goals. It will review your current asset allocations and investment performance. This is a document to review periodically to make sure you are on track with your investment goals.

A New Mindset: Investing with Impact

Laura inherited her investment dollars. "I got my money from my dad and my values from my mom," she says with a smile. She buys her clothes at thrift stores, lives in a modest apartment, and rides her bike around the city. She doesn't really want people to know she has money. As a privileged white woman with assets, she works to find ways to support BIPOC-based businesses. She volunteers her time with groups that do impact investing. She made a decision to invest outside the stock market and in small entrepreneurial endeavors like a minority-owned solar company and a clothing company that makes ethical and planet-friendly clothing. She also just moved her banking operations to a local minority-owned bank in her city as she wants to support their efforts to build community.

Investment in the societal and financial sense traditionally meant that your money makes money; that is, investing is the chance to increase your wealth. Think about the wealthy who use investments as passive income. This often means sending it off to the stock market or other capital markets to increase the bottom lines of businesses and corporations. A fundamental shift in using money as a tool is to realize investments are not just for generating returns but they are also for shaping the world in which we live! Consider what positive impact you would like your investment to have. What non-financial benefits are important to you?

Investing is an important part of our money journey because of the impact it has on our world. If we view investing from the narrow perspective of risk and return, a tree is worth more dead than alive. Think of a tree—a living tree in the forest—living in an ecosystem with soil, organisms, plants, and animals. It's a complex relationship. Mother Nature gives us this tree as a gift of Her generosity.

However, when viewed from the narrow viewpoint of conventional finance, a tree is worth more commercially as cut lumber. Neither the company that harvests the lumber, nor the consumers who purchase the lumber, pay the forest for her generosity, or consider the damage to the other plants, animals, soil, and water that make up that ecosystem. We are using the Earth's resources but not considering Her contribution to the financial equation. When we consider the larger picture of investing, we are making a choice to listen to the soul self, and to pay

When we consider the larger picture of investing, we are making a choice to listen to the soul self, and to pay attention to, care for, and honor the Earth. This is part of our money journey.

attention to, care for, and honor the Earth. This is part of our money journey.

It's my hope that the investments I make will positively impact our communities and our world, instead of continuing the old model of extraction which ignores or neglects the true cost of those resources. As Autumn is when we harvest one year's crops to make room for the next, I want to take my resources and plant something new.

What Is Impact Investing?

Consider the definition by Investopedia.com: "Impact investing is an investment strategy that aims to generate specific, beneficial, social or environmental effects in addition to financial gains. Impact investments may take the form of numerous asset classes and may result in many specific outcomes. The point of impact investing is to use money and investment capital for positive social results."[97] This definition allows us to consider the planet, people, and place in our investing decisions.

Many of us feel, since we are not in the top 10 percent of income earners, that what we do doesn't matter. But the fact is, we (in the United States) are a nation of wealth holders. Everyone who belongs to a pension fund, belongs to a teachers' retirement system, supports a university foundation, contributes to a community foundation, or is a beneficiary of a public service retirement fund, is a wealth holder. It's time to take responsibility for where and how we are investing.

For example, in the 1980s there was a groundswell of support at American universities to divest university endowment portfolios from American businesses doing business in South Africa.[98] Students were protesting apartheid and influenced these large funds to divest of stocks in companies that were supporting the South African apartheid system.

Socially responsible investing's origins in the United States began in the eighteenth century.[99] Methodists and Quakers advised members to avoid investing in the slave trade, smuggling, liquor, tobacco, or gambling. Eventually, in 1928, a group in Boston founded the first publicly offered fund, the Pioneer Fund, which had similar restrictions. These early investing strategies applied by these groups were intended to eliminate so-called sin industries in their investment portfolios. More recently, in 1977, Pax World Fund launched the first socially responsible investment fund, and since then, impact investing has been gaining recognition and market share.

In general, impact investing is an investment strategy that attempts to allow an investor to "do well by doing good" in the language of the industry. Investors want to consider the environment, corporate behavior, and the social costs and benefits of the investment. Historically, one approach used to move toward sustainable or impact investing was the exclusion or negative screening method: for example, not investing in fossil fuels because of the impact on the environment. Some common exclusionary investments avoid companies that promote gambling, alcohol, chemicals, firearms, or for-profit prisons. Impact investing could also limit investments, for example, in countries with a history of human rights abuses. Additionally, it could exclude companies that score low on environmental, social, or governance factors compared with other companies in the industry.

There is also positive screening, which identifies companies contributing to positive environmental or social change for investment.

Terms used in the financial industry are *socially responsible investing* (SRI) and *environment, social, and governance* (ESG) investing. I like the term *impact investing*.

All investments have an impact; let's think about and align our money with investments that have a positive social benefit. We must consider not just the company and the ROI, but also the impacted stakeholders like customers, company employees, the supply chain, and, of course, the communities impacted by the business. We need to consider both the financial and the non-financial return of our investment.

We also need to consider the time horizon for our investment. How quickly or how patiently do you want your money to work? In their recent publication, *Community Investment Funds,* Brian Beckon, Amy Cortese, Janice Shade, and Michael H. Shuman share this perspective: "What exactly is the standard for impact investing? Those of us preparing this volume believe that, at a minimum, it should be place-based investments that are both patient and catalytic. Too many impact investors are comfortable supporting global companies that match or even better the rates of return from Wall Street. Patient capital, in contrast, seeks to create positive impact, even if it means a lower rate of return." [100]

When we invest thoughtfully, with a focus on creating a just, sustainable world, I consider that changing financing and financing change. It's a wonderful way to have an impact!

There is evidence of change in the air. In his book, *Powering Prosperity: A Citizen's Guide to Shaping the 21st Century,* author Indranil Ghosh shares the growing trend that sustainable investing has moved into the mainstream markets, saying, "It's a growing trend, especially among women and the younger millennial generation, to select investment managers that can deliver both competitive returns and positive social outcomes."[101]

I am not a financial planner, investment adviser, or business consultant. I am a global citizen, family member, author, and artist who cares about this world and thinks that using money to make the world a better place makes sense. There are ways to invest in things we understand and to find simple, uncomplicated ways to use our money wisely.

There are a variety of ways to support small businesses, regenerative agriculture, sustainable land development, and impactful global efforts. At this point in your journey, it's now up to you to find the types of investments that support your values.

One of the directories that could assist you in the process can be found at Invest with Values, an online resource for the investor wanting to align their money and their values.[102] They have an extensive online directory of up-to-date investment opportunities including local banking, community investing, sustainable and responsible investing, and impact investing with purpose-driven companies and social entrepreneurs. Additionally, there are suggestions for books, articles, and websites about money and sustainable investing.

Finding a Values Aligned Financial Adviser

Financial planning seems like something only professionals (like financial advisers and CPAs) do. But truthfully, we are all responsible for our own money path.

There is so much information on finance, investments, money, and the economy that it's easy to get overwhelmed. There are books, newspapers, magazines, newsletters, blogs, organizations, companies, and institutions that deal with these money issues daily. There are experts, specialists, and authorities abounding. The biggest issue is that, even with those resources available, it is still up to us to take control, manage, and decide how to create a kind, just world with our money.

So how do you find a financial adviser that you trust, like, and who understands you?

There are a variety of types of financial advisers: coaches and counselors, credit consultants, and budget counselors. There are sales-based advisers who have products and are paid commissions to sell various investment products. There are financial planners, offering advice on portfolio allocation; there is typically a charge for their services. There are fee-only advisers; they typically charge a percentage of the assets under management.

As you decide who you want to work with, there are a variety of articles online about questions to ask as you interview financial advisers. Make sure you ask about credentials, costs, fees, specialization, or focus, and how they work. Get clear on communication, how often, and where you might be meeting. If you are interested in learning more about impact investing, make sure to ask about what options are available, and how their firm, office, or business handles ESG or SRI investments. Consider writing out a list of questions to ask as you interview potential financial advisers.[103]

As you move your investment focus to impact investing, also ask if the adviser has screening tools that align values with investment opportunities. Does the financial adviser have knowledge or experience with the United Nations Sustainable Development Goals, ESG, or SRI investments? What is the personal philosophy of the adviser with regard to impact investing and using money as a tool for regenerative or restorative capital? Discussions about money, especially your money, should include lots of interaction.

As you consider your investments, also consider the following: Is an accumulation of wealth your goal? Or perhaps, using a wider lens, and your bigger vision, what kind of world do you want to create with your money?

Investing is only one tool on your journey to create a just, regenerative world. However, it's worth spending time and effort to be able to make choices and decisions that align with your purpose and your intentions. The following exercise will help clarify your current situation.

EXERCISE

Assembling Your Current Financial Portfolio

In Chapter 7, you calculated your net worth by listing your assets and liabilities. Now we are going to examine in more detail your actual assets and investments. This process may take a bit of time, it may trigger some emotional responses, or it may take some detective work to find where money might be hidden, such as in an account you haven't looked at in a while. If you have a financial adviser, reach out and request a recent statement.

1. *Review your financial goals.*
2. *Open up your bank, investment, or online statements. Spend time looking at where you have money invested. Look at your 401K, your retirement plans, and where you are invested in the stock market. How does this make you feel? Assemble a list of your current portfolio assets: Here is a common way to list your investments:*
    a. *Cash and cash alternatives*
    b. *Stocks*
    c. *Bonds*
    d. *Real estate*
    e. *Other investments*
3. *Consider your investment objectives: Are you saving to buy a house, investing for growth, or for cash flow? These are wonderful questions to consider with your partner or a financial adviser.*

Congratulate yourself on pulling together your list of investments. Make a list of the next steps, put a date of completion on each step, and put those dates in your calendar. Celebrate yourself and your efforts!

Affirmations

- I am a wise money steward, using my money and my spirit to create a just, sustainable world.
- I am grateful and pleased to use my resources to invest in a healthy planet.
- I accept and appreciate this path of investing with love and gratitude.

Chapter 15
Conclusion and Next Steps

Indeed, the purpose of an economy should be to enable the conditions in which all people can achieve the highest possible states of well-being.
—Mark Anielski[104]

Re-visioning Money, Finances, and Economics in Today's World

The world continues to evolve regarding money, finance, and investing. I continue to be dazed by the complex world of economics. Even with our current capitalistic system, I am still dedicated to a just, sustainable, kind, thriving world. It's the world I want to live in; it's the world I want my kids and grandkids to live in, and it's the world that I want to leave for future generations.

This requires new and perhaps risky thinking. New insights and actions endanger the safety and security of our prior assumptions. But indeed, we bring our hope and pray that our insights and action will bring radical transformation to our world. It's our collective action that will turn us from unlimited growth and expansion of the *Me, More, Mine* focus to preservation of our current resources and a deeper relationship with each other and Mother Earth.

We are each a precious part of the web of life. You matter, and your decisions matter. It behooves us to gather to remember, knowing that all of life is sacred. All of life is sacred: the air we breathe, the water that supports life, the land we need to nurture and protect, our brothers and sisters, human, animal, fish, and fowl, especially the Earth Herself.

We need to blend the world of money and investing with our inner sacred selves. It's time for a breakthrough to connect our sacred selves with the money we earn, spend, save, and invest with the place and time in which we live, and how we choose to be in this world of money and finance.

Let's shift our financial systems from a focus on profit toward a just, kind, regenerative, life-giving Earth system for humans and nature. Constructing a new economy is one of the most important tasks of our time. Society desperately needs a replacement for our current extractive, exploitative, financial system. You and I are the imaginal cells of the new future we are creating with our money.

Nature teaches us that caterpillars don't reproduce. After eating many times its weight, a caterpillar creates a chrysalis. Inside the chrysalis, its cells actually dissolve; once dissolved, these imaginal cells transform the cell soup into a butterfly. This messy, biological process creates new life, beauty, function, and interconnectedness with the environment. Like the caterpillar, we can each bring our own beauty to the world.

You and I are the imaginal cells of the new future we are creating with our money.

As we honor our relationship with money to include our sacred self, we also honor the Divinity in each other. We can transform the financial system with which we interact so that it too can become just, kind, and regenerative. By adding caring, compassion, and kinship to our money flow, we impact the world in beautiful ways. We are the imaginal cells for a societal transformation. We are the midwives of the new financial and societal way of being. We are hospice workers who encourage and witness as the old capitalist system dies.

I do think we are moving from the old thinking of *Me, More, Mine* to a healthier framework of *Us, We, and the Earth.* I believe we can move through our financial seasons to grow a new way of life. It's an exciting time to be alive. Together we can create an ecologically sustainable, collaborative, restorative ecosystem that is socially and culturally diverse, allowing all systems, people, and places to prosper.

It's time to think outside the box, see differently, acknowledge the old ways are not working, and search for a new story that includes all of humanity, the Earth, and all beings and creatures of nature. It's remembering that you and I are each distinctly unique beings, designed and created within the billions of galaxies and that we have in our bodies billions of cells that are alive and help us live. We live in a world that is so diverse, abundant with plants, animals, insects, birds, and grains of sand, we as humans cannot measure them. There is a cosmic order, a universe, a power we call Divine. It contains and commands the substance and performance of life itself. Unlike money, it cannot be measured, calculated, accumulated, or verified. There is no way to calculate, count, quantify, rate, or weigh this essence; but without a doubt, it exists.

We are fundamentally connected and supported by a Divine power and a Divine purpose. The sacred and the secular are not separate. They are linked, tied together as building blocks for our new world. We can do something about the destruction of the environment; we can do something about starvation; and we can do something about racism, but only if we act through the lens of inclusivity, kindness, and cooperation. It must include a recognition of the Divine not necessarily through a religious lens, though it can include all religions.

Rather, it is a recognition that we are finding common ground in recognition of Divinity within each of us.

It is time to build a soul-filled, inclusive society, that honors the life force of spirit and diversity in everyone and everything, honoring the world as our common space where everyone can thrive. By healing our money story, by finding ways to deploy our money in focused caring ways, and by changing our money from *Me, More, Mine* to *Us, We, and the Earth*, we can make big impacts on our lives and the lives of people we love and the rest of the world.

As we finish our journey through this book, we can look at it as an initiation: the act of entering an experience or sphere of activity previously unknown to us. The closing of initiation is the death of the old self and the rebirth of the new self. We have faced the journey of money, and now we are new and different, spiritually and financially.

Writing this book has been my initiation into the world of finance and connecting it with my spiritual life. Together, we have looked at the paradigm shift from *Me, More, Mine* to *Us, We, and the Earth.* We have looked deeply at our money beliefs and money story. By healing our money story, by setting our intentions, by taking time to connect with our money and our finances, we are changed.

This rite of passage recognizes the efforts, the wisdom we've gained, the courage, and the determination with which we have applied ourselves to this task. We also know, although we are complete with this task, our work is never really done. The spiritual practice of personal transformation and the daily requirements of money management do not end. We are now better able to perform each task with kindness and generosity, remembering our creative vision of a just, sustainable world.

Blessings to you, dear reader.

Concluding Money Ritual–Death, Growth, and Rebirth

Preparation: This ritual is a rite of transition, an opportunity to bless and integrate the changes in your money journey. We die to our old selves, we become our new, Spirit-inspired selves.

For this ritual, you may want to invite others as witness to your transformation.

Prepare your space or an altar for a celebration. Bring flowers or other items to decorate your ceremonial place. Place each of the following on your prepared space: First, select a rock and a symbol of your old money self (for example, your old money story). Second, bring money and a token of your growth (your completed net worth statement). Third, bring an essential oil (pine or one of your favorite essential oils) and write a brief vision of your plans for your healed financial future (your vision statement of a just, sustainable world).

Begin with deep calming breaths. Imagine breathing in Divine Light, flowing into your heart and all over your body. Allow all concerns or inner chaos to be released with each out breath. When you are ready, begin the ritual.

Opening Prayer:

> *I call upon the love of Spirit, God/Goddess, our Divine Beloved. As I die to the old way of being with money, I celebrate a new, healthy, divinely supported and guided way of being in the world. Source of all goodness, I thank you for Your inspiration and wisdom.*

Ritual of Death, Growth, and Rebirth.:

With silence, hold your rock and symbol of your old story and say, "*As I reflect on my past relationship with money, I allow this part of my life to be given back to the Earth. I thank these experiences for leading me to a new way of being. I bless this rock and my old money self and allow this to be part of the Earth.*"

With silence, hold your cash and symbol of your growth and say, "*I am growing in my awareness of the power of my spirit and using money as a tool. I give thanks for this journey of self-discovery. I am supported and guided in all my money and life endeavors.*"

In silence, anoint yourself with the oil, anointing your hands, your heart, your throat, and your forehead. Hold your symbol of your future vision and say, "*I bless myself and my unfolding future. I give thanks for the abundance, blessings, and possibilities for a just, kind, regenerative future for me, humanity, the Earth, and all beings.*"

Silent meditation.

Closing prayer:

> *Great Mystery, I am grateful for the healing of my money journey and for money as a Divine Source of life and a blessing. I stand before You, ready to use money to serve the highest and best transformation for the good of all, humanity, Mother Earth, and all Her beings of the plant, animal, and mineral realms. I am grateful for the Earth that sustains us and pray for balance to be restored. I recognize my Divine Light and now allow myself and my money to shine as I now help create a just, sustainable world. Blessed Be, and So It Is.*

End of Ritual

Let's Stay Connected!

Thank you for joining me on this journey to the heart of our spirit and our finances. As we move forward to a new, kind, just sustainable world, let's support each other.

I would love to speak at your group, organization, podcast or show! Please reach out at: gcm@genevievecmitchell.com

Let's stay connected!

- Visit my Website at: genevievecmitchell.com
- Follow me on Facebook: https://www.facebook.com/genevieve.chavezmitchell
- Find me on LinkedIn: https://www.linkedin.com/in/genevieve-chavez-mitchell/

Appendix 1
Tools for Healing Your Money Story

There are a variety of ways to heal ourselves, physically, emotionally, mentally, and spiritually. I want to share some of the approaches and techniques I have used over the years. Use what works for you. Emotional pain around money is very real. It requires care, gentleness, kindness, and time. This is not a get-fixed-quick process. Healing money wounds is a bit like healing a broken heart—you can't see the pain or the changes from the outside, but it's a very real process on the inside.

The tools that have been very helpful for me are ritual, walking, forgiveness, and the Emotional Freedom Technique. I hope you will consider adding them to your daily repertoire of practices to engage in a healthier, emotionally healed relationship with money. Once you work with the tools of walking, forgiveness, and the EFT, it's time to write and rewrite your money stories.

Healing Your Money Story

These journaling exercises are offered to allow you to open up to the stories, beliefs, and ideology that frame your relationship with money. By exploring these questions, you will often recognize how to do things differently.

Journaling Questions to Get Started

Do you feel like you are blocked on the issue of money? Please let go of the idea that you are blocked. Rather say, "I am experiencing the energy of being blocked. I now lovingly and with great kindness allow the energy and flow of money to heal my money story." Be kind to yourself as you journal these questions.

- What was your money story growing up?
- How do you feel about money?
- Do you like your relationship with money?
- Is there fear, angst, or sadness about money?
- Are there feelings of overwhelm or distress when you think about your financial situation?
- Does thinking about money trigger anxiety, fear, or worry?
- Are your money records messy or disorganized, or are you way behind on putting things in order?
- Do you know how much debt you have?
- Do you have a plan to get out of that debt?
- Do you worry about running out of money?
- Do you know what's in your retirement funds? What is your money situation now?
- Would you like to feel more responsible and in charge of your money?
- How can you add more kindness, compassion, and love into your relationship with money?

Ritual

Ritual has been with us as long as humans have been around. It may be something you know, or it may be something you create. But celebrations of all types are rituals. For example, praying before a meal, going to church, or attending funeral rites are common rituals. We create rituals when we infuse the energy of the sacred into the doing of an event.

Rituals elevate ordinary time and space to become holy and sacred. Ritual is about setting intention, space, time, and focus for being fully present and clearing the mind.

Another reminder is that rituals and prayers are *not* the paths; they are reminders that there *is* a Divine path.

One way to learn about rituals is to attend them, in church, in group gatherings, at liturgy or religious events, and in a circle of people you trust who want to celebrate. Rituals can be used to honor someone or consecrate an event, a theme, or a place. In doing ritual, you become a sacred space holder, a vessel of the Mystery that enriches you and all you touch. There is an enchanting alchemy of you, intention, and Spirit that unfolds as you plan your ritual.

Walking

The benefits of walking are numerous. Walking alone is a gift to yourself that doesn't cost anything, is available to you easily, and fits into a busy schedule. Of course, you exercise and move your body, which is wonderful. However, having a regularly scheduled time in your day to leave the rest of the world behind allows you to be open to the healing energy of open air, nature, neighbors, the sky, and the sun, and to be alone with your own thoughts.

I have been a walker my whole life; it's my basic mental health tool. Yes, there are physical benefits, but mostly I walk to sort out confusion, ponder solutions, allow ideas to percolate, and soothe whatever challenges are pressing on my heart. I hope you might consider taking a walk today, maybe right now, as a gift to yourself. There are short walks, long walks, and walks with those you love. You can go on hikes, and pilgrimages, walk labyrinths, walk on city streets, walk in the desert, on the beach, or in the mountains. As Julia Cameron says in her book *The Vein of Gold: A Journey to Your Creative Heart,* "...when we walk into the outer world, we are moved into the inner one as well."[105] Walking is a wonderful way to sort through whatever feelings, challenges, or emotions come your way.

Forgiveness

Forgiveness is a process of inner work to let go and move on. It's a decision. In forgiving, we release blame, resentment, revenge, and the need to be right. In her book, *Forgiveness Workbook: A Step by Step Guide*, Eileen Barker reminds us of what forgiveness is and is not:

What Forgiveness Is:

- Forgiveness is taking back your power.
- Forgiveness is taking responsibility for how you feel.
- Forgiveness is for you and not the offender.
- Forgiveness is about your healing and not about the people who hurt you.
- Forgiveness is a trainable skill.
- Forgiveness is becoming a hero instead of a victim.
- Forgiveness is a choice.

What Forgiveness Is Not:

- Forgiveness is not condoning unkindness.
- Forgiveness is not forgetting that something painful happened.
- Forgiveness is not excusing poor behavior.
- Forgiveness does not have to be an otherworldly or religious experience.
- Forgiveness is not denying or minimizing your hurt.
- Forgiveness does not mean reconciling with the offender.

- Forgiveness does not mean you give up having feelings about what occurred.

The money decisions I have made have not always worked out well. My husband and I invested a large amount of money with a start-up technology company in our community. I was quite impressed with the concept of being able to help many people with a technology that could be provided at a low cost. The possibilities for scaling the business appeared exceptional. I liked the CEO, the tech team had impressive work histories, and there were already investors who had put money into the business.

We went into a meeting to learn more. We asked questions, asked for financial information, and looked at upcoming contracts. Everything seemed in order. So, we invested.

The business needed more money, the CEO was always on the verge of a big investor coming in, and the contracts were always *almost* signed. So, we invested more money. We kept asking for information and reports, but communication was sporadic and infrequent. Then, over time, the CEO had health issues: major, long-term, debilitating health challenges. Unable to maintain her health and the company operations, financial reports were not forthcoming, the contracts were not signed, the business eventually failed, and we lost a large chunk of change.

I always felt that this loss was my fault. In my enthusiasm for the project and the people, we had not done an adequate job of due diligence and we invested way too much in one business.

After a time, I recognized I needed to forgive myself, the CEO, and other employees of this company who I knew personally. My heart and my pride were both deeply hurt by this failure. I took time to process my feelings of frustration, disappointment, and betrayal. I prayed, I meditated, I listened to forgiveness meditations, and I used the EFT to tap through all the feelings of shame, inadequacy, and defeat. It took time, but this was a big lesson for me, and it allowed me to move forward and release this very painful mistake.

Because life is challenging and there are work difficulties, family problems, betrayals, and financial setbacks, blame is often the place we go to park those problems. It was her fault, his fault, their fault; it was someone's action, decision, or response that was the problem. But placing blame doesn't fix the issue. Forgiveness is a way to unlock the need to blame and allows us to let go of the guilt, sadness, or other feelings that no longer serve us.

It takes courage to forgive. It can require baby steps of acknowledging the pain, sitting with the grief, and allowing forgiveness into your heart. Also, remember that often the person we most need to forgive is ourselves.

EXERCISE

Forgiveness Meditation

Jack Kornfield teaches the three directions of forgiveness. In his wonderful teaching on forgiveness,[106] he invites us into a transformative forgiveness meditation.

The first direction is the forgiveness of others. He asks us to identify the ways we have hurt or harmed others, to remember that time, feel the sadness or regret. Then ask forgiveness from those we have hurt.

The second direction is forgiveness for yourself. There are so many ways we have hurt, betrayed, or abandoned ourselves. In this meditation, we extend forgiveness to ourselves for all the ways and times that we acted from fear, pain, or confusion. Then you forgive yourself.

Finally, the third direction of forgiveness is forgiveness for those who have hurt or harmed you. Normally, this is what we think of when we want to forgive: we forgive others. When identifying those who have hurt or harmed you, begin by feeling that sorrow. Then proceed, "I now remember the many ways others have hurt or harmed me, wounded me, out of fear, pain, confusion, and anger. I have carried this pain in my heart too long. To the extent that I am ready, I offer them forgiveness. To those who have caused me harm, I offer my forgiveness, I forgive you."[107]

Be kind to yourself as you engage in forgiveness practice. It's a wonderful way to let go of the past and bring a new outlook and perspective to your internal state. I personally have found this particular meditation very useful. You might consider doing it daily for a week or a month or do it regularly to release blame, shame, burden, and pain.

EFT

Emotional Freedom Technique (or EFT) is an emotional healing technique using fingertips to tap on acupuncture points on the body.

Basically, EFT is a tapping technique that balances the energy meridians in the body that become disrupted when we think about or experience emotionally disturbing situations. After using EFT, oftentimes the upset or intensity of the situation is relieved. The memory or circumstance stays but the emotional charge is gone. Typically, the result is lasting and is often accompanied by a more positive outlook on the situation.

Based on the ancient principles of acupuncture, EFT is a simple tapping procedure that gently realigns the body's energy system, without the discomfort of needles. EFT incorporates an emotional element into the healing process, addressing unresolved emotional issues as a likely cause of physical disease, psychological dysfunction, and personal performance limits.

EFT evolved from Thought Field Therapy (TFT)[108] and is part of the widely used Meridian Tapping Techniques (MTT).[109] Developed by Gary Craig in 1995, Craig pioneered a discovery statement that "The cause of all negative emotions is a disruption in the body's energy system."[110] A disruption can be grief, a trauma, a fear, or a memory. Craig learned that by tapping specific acupuncture points on the body, clients were relieved of emotional problems. Since those early days, many new instructors have spread EFT through books, articles, and courses. EFT is easily learned, easily done, and very effective.

EXERCISE

Tapping with EFT

Begin by tapping on the outside of the fleshy part of the hand (karate chop point). Start with the set up phrase while tapping on the karate chop point.

- *Even though __________(state your problem here), I deeply and completely love and accept myself.*

Tap at each point and state your reminder phrase (see next page for tapping points). Your reminder phrase is a short description of the problem on each point while tapping five to seven times on each point. Remember to take a deep breath after the last tapping point.

Example Money Set Up and Reminder Phrases

- Even though I feel so sad about money, I deeply and completely love and accept myself. Reminder phrase: "I'm sad."

- Even though I feel like such a failure about money, I deeply and completely love and accept myself. Reminder phrase: "Failure"
- Even though I am scared to look at my money, I deeply and completely love and accept myself. Reminder phrase: "Scared"

The Sequence

1. *Eyebrow (beginning of eyebrow, just above and to one side of the nose)*
2. *Side of eye (on bone bordering outside of eye)*
4. *Under eye (on bone under pupil)*
5. *Under nose*
6. *Chin point (between chin and bottom lip)*
7. *Collarbone point (small dip underneath collarbone near sternum)*
8. *Under the arm*
9. *Top of head*

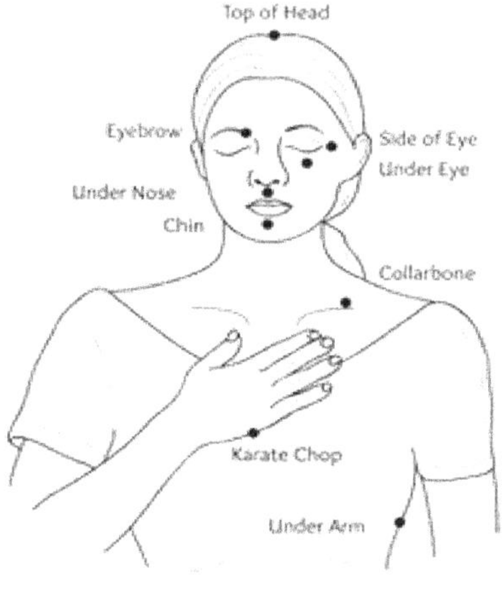

EFT Tapping Points

It's as easy as tapping these points. If you are intensely in the emotion, no need to say anything, just tap! You can tap with either hand, either side, or both sides. It's good to tap all the points, but just tapping the karate chop or other single point can be very helpful. You can do this daily or hourly if you are feeling very intense about anything.

EFT is a wonderful way to release any emotional discomfort about any topic, relationship, or distress you may be feeling.

Living Room Conversation with Your Pain

Use this exercise when you feel confused, hurt, or bewildered by a feeling, experience, or situation.

Imagine yourself in a beautiful living room or perhaps a library of a special place, like an old castle. There is a warm fire in the fireplace, beautiful art and books on the wall, and two comfortable chairs, with a sweet table between them, ready with tea for two.

Invite your pain, confusion, situation, or challenge to sit in the second chair. Get cozy and begin a conversation. Here are a few questions to ask: What is it that you are trying to teach me? What is it that I need to learn from this experience? Is there a different way to look at this situation than I can see right now? What is it that I don't know that I don't know? What is the best way to take care of myself right now? What is my best response? What else do I need to know?

Take some time to write out your experience and new understandings.

This exercise is helpful in giving insight in a gentle, non-judgmental way.

Appendix 2
Lists of Exercises and Rituals

List of Exercises

List of Rituals

Appendix 3
Books Worth Reading

Books about Money

Eisenstein, Charles. *Sacred Economics: Money, Gift and Society in the Age of Transition* (Berkeley: Evolver Editions, 2011).

Emerson, Jed, *The Purpose of Capital: Elements of Impact, Financial Flows and Natural Being* (Blended Value Group, 2018).

Firpo, Janine, *Activate Your Money: Invest to Grow Your Wealth and Build a Better World* (New Jersey: John Wiley and Sons, 2021).

Mackey, John and Sisodia, Raj, *Conscious Capitalism: Liberating the Heroic Spirit of Business* (United States: Harvard Business School Publishing, 2014).

Shuman, Michael, *Put Your Money Where Your Life Is: How to Invest Locally Using Self-Directed IRAs and Solo 401(k)s* (California: Berret-Koehler, 2020).

Simon, Morgan, *Real Impact: The New Economics of Social Change: Using Impact Investing to Change the World* (PublicAffairs, 2017).

Tessler, Bari, *The Art of Money: A Life-Changing Guide to Financial Happiness* (Berkeley: Parallax Press, 2016).

Twist, Lynne, The Soul of Money: Reclaiming the Wealth of Our Inner Resources (New York: W.W. Norton & Company, 2003).

Books about Spirituality

Brach, Tara, *Radical Acceptance: Embracing Your Life with the Heart of a Buddha* (New York: Bantam Dell, 2003).

Don, Megan, *The New Divine Feminine: Spiritual Evolution for a Woman's Soul* (Llewellyn Worldwide, Limited, 2016).

Dupre, Louis, and Wiseman, James, eds., *Light from Light: An Anthology of Christian Mysticism* (New York: Paulist Press, 2001).

Mitchell, Genevieve and Key, Anne, *Prayers to the Goddess: A Moon Cycle Devotion,* (New Mexico: Goddess In, 2019).

Monaghan, Patricia, *The Goddess Path: Myths, Invocations & Rituals* (St. Paul: Llewellyn Publications, 2004).

Neu, Diann *Women's Rites: Feminist Liturgies for Life's Journey* (Cleveland: The Pilgrim Press, 2003).

Palmer, Parker, *A Hidden Wholeness: The Journey Toward an Undivided Life* (San Francisco: Jossey-Bass, 2004).

Starhawk and Valentine, Hilary, *The Twelve Wild Swans: A Journey to the Realm of Magic Healing, and Action* (United States: HarperCollins, 2000).

Starr, Mirabai, *Wild Mercy: Living the Fierce and Tender Wisdom of the Women Mystics* (Colorado: Sounds True, 2019).

Stein, Diane, ed., *The Goddess Celebrates: An Anthology of Women's Rituals* (Freedom CA: The Crossing Press, 1991).

Acknowledgments

I offer a deep bow of gratitude to the land of my ancestors and the heritage in which I was raised. These have shaped my view of the world, one connected to the earth and based on community and connection.

I owe much appreciation to the modern teachers, activists, and writers who have inspired, informed and motivated me to learn and explore the connection between money, consciousness, and spirituality. Thanks to Lynne Twist, Jed Emerson, Kristin Hull, Janine Firpo, Charles Eisenstein, Woody Tasch, Lawrence Ford, Valerie Brown, Morgan Simon, Michael Shuman, and Eva Yazhari.

I want to give credit to Austin Kleon, who inspired me with his suggestion that I write the book on money and spirituality that I couldn't find to read. To Jane Midgely who shepherded me to get me to a place where the idea of a book took hold. To Pam Slim for valuable book coaching support, thank you! To all the clients, students, workshop participants, and mastermind colleagues, thank you. To my friends and colleagues at Women in Publishing, especially Alexa Bigwarfe for her generous teachings. To my cohorts and colleagues at Invest for Better, especially Janine Firpo, Ellen Remmer, Babbie Jacobs, Theresa Mitchell, and Eileen Frieberger. To Cayelin Castell and the Venus Alchemy group, thank you. To my National Association of Women Business Owner sisters, Women Who Make a Difference, and the lovely community at Albuquerque Center for Spiritual Leadership I offer deep gratitude.

To the women who agreed to be interviewed for their perspectives, especially Laina Raveendran Greene, Sharon Bowes, Cayelin Castell, and Babbie Jacobs. To early readers of the manuscript, Anna Paradox,

Elsie Maio, Theresa Mitchell, Katherine Longi, and Tascha Yoder, I am grateful for all your comments. For handholding, editing, and publishing expertise thanks to Tascha Yoder, Carly Fahey Dima, Laurie Knight, Michelle Vanderpas, and the team at Gracepoint Publishing.

For my Gladiolous gal pals, Chris Sanders, Amy Jones, Anne Luna, and especially Anna Paradox, an early reader, editor, and friend, for all her help and advice. I deeply appreciate my soul sisters, Ena Pearl, for discernment advice, Tami Brunk for accountability and celestial support, Caya Tanski for our long and fruitful friendship, and Elsie Maio for encouragement and marketing support. Big gratitude to coach extraordinaire, Paul Zelizer for ongoing friendship and encouragement. For my dearest Kathryn Ravenwood, for being my thinking pal, my travel buddy, and my ongoing cheerleader, boundless thanks.

Finally, to my big, beautiful family, Luke, Emily, Eliora, Caleb, Aaron, Alex, Jacob, Rita, Alice, Jude, Adam, and my brothers, Jim, John, Paul, and Lawrence and their families, thank you for being you. My deepest, most heartfelt appreciation and gratitude go to my husband Paul, I love you.

End Notes

Chapter 1

1. My husband, Paul, and I have been married since 1984. This money story is ours but told from my perspective.
2. https://www.episcopalchurch.org/glossary/philadelphia-eleven-the/. The Philadelphia Eleven were the eleven women who were ordained priests at the Church of the Advocate, Philadelphia, on the feast of St. Mary and St. Martha, July 29, 1974, two years before General Convention authorized the ordination of women.

Chapter 2

3. Anne Lamott, *Help. Thanks. Wow.* (New York: Riverhead Books, 2012), 2.
4. Adapted from Genevieve C. Mitchell and Anne Key *Prayers to the Goddess: A Moon Cycle Devotion* (New Mexico: Goddess In, 2019), 131.

Chapter 3

5. Sallie McFague, *Blessed Are the Consumers: Climate Change and the Practice of Restraint* (Fortress Press: 2013), 6, 7.

Chapter 4

6. Tara Brach, *Radical Acceptance: Embracing Your Life with the Heart of a Buddha* (New York: Bantam Dell,2004), 53.

Chapter 5

7. Bernard Lietaer, *The Mystery of Money: Beyond Greed and Scarcity* (Munich: Riemann Verlag, 2000), 41.
8. Joan Goodnick Westenholz, "Goddesses of the Ancient Near East, 3000-1000 BC" in Goodison, Lucy & Morris, Christine, eds., *Ancient Goddesses* (British Museum Press, 1998), 71.
9. https://en.wikipedia.org/wiki/Pythia.
10. I want to recognize the great civilizations of India, the Orient, the rich history of Africa, and the native people of North and South America. This book, however, is based mostly on Western, Judeo-Christian thought.
11. https://en.wikipedia.org/wiki/Witch-hunt.
12. https://www.history.com/this-day-in-history/abigail-adams-urges-husband-to-remember-the-ladies.

13. https://en.wikipedia.org/wiki/Married_Women's_Property_Acts_in_the_United_States.
14. https://www.reference.com/business-finance/difference-between-formal-informal-sectors-aab0ae9eb69681af.
15. https://www.oxfam.org/en/not-all-gaps-are-created-equal-true-value-care-work.
16. https://www.forbes.com/sites/maggiegermano/2020/09/22/how-women-can-change-the-world-with-their-money-choices/?sh=4a1aa1086138.
17. https://www.forbes.com/sites/maggiegermano/2020/09/22/how-women-can-change-the-world-with-their-money-choices/?sh=4a1aa1086138.
18. https://www.nawbo.org/sites/nawbo/files/Merrill Lynch Age Wave Women Study.pdf.
19. https://www.fool.com/research/women-in-investing-research/.
20. https://philanthropywomen.org/research/women-give-more-from-less/.
21. https://www.earthday.org/womens-empowerment-is-key-to-reducing-climate-change.
22. https://www.un.org/sustainabledevelopment/gender-equality/.
23. https://www.un.org/sustainabledevelopment/gender-equality/.
24. https://www.un.org/sustainabledevelopment/gender-equality/.

Chapter 6

25. https://www.worlddata.info/currencies/.
26. https://slowmoney.org/.
27. Lynne Twist, *The Soul of Money: Reclaiming the Wealth of Our Inner Resources* (New York: W.W. Norton & Company), 48-55.

Chapter 7

28. https://sdgs.un.org/goals.
29. https://www.investopedia.com/articles/retirement/10/estate-planning-checklist.asp.

Chapter 8

30. https://money.usnews.com/money/personal-finance/family-finance/articles/worthwhile-online-personal-finance-courses.
31. Dave Ramsey's Solutions, http://ramseysolutions.com.
32. Suze Orman, http://www.suzeorman.com.
33. https://www.merriam-webster.com/dictionary/credit.
34. https://www.consumerfinance.gov/consumer-tools/credit-reports-and-scores/.
35. https://www.carpro.com/blog/when-you-owe-more-on-your-car-than-its-worth.

36. https://www.newyorkfed.org/microeconomics/hhdc.html.

37. DeForest B. Soaries, Jr., *Say Yes to No Debt: 12 Steps to Financial Freedom* (United States of America: Zondervan, 2015), 19.

38. Bari Tessler, *The Art of Money: A Life Changing Guide to Financial Happiness* (Berkeley: Parallax Press, 2016), 151.

Part Four Introduction

39. https://bostonimpact.org/.

40. https://rsfsocialfinance.org/vision/how-we-work/.

41. https://www.kiva.org/.

42. https://homewise.org/.

43. Poem: *This is My Father's World* by Maltbie Davenport Babcock, 1901, adapted by Genevieve Chavez Mitchell.

Chapter 9

44. Frederick Buechner, *Wishful Thinking: A Seeker's ABC* (San Fransisco: Harper, 1993), 118-19

45. Richard N. Bolles, *What Color Is your Parachute: Meaningful Work and Career Success* (Ten Speed Press: 2022).

46. https://www.forbes.com/sites/sap/2022/04/04/3-global-trends-affecting-your-employees.

47. For a deep dive into meaning and the workplace see Mark Bryan, Julia Cameron, and Catherine A. Allen, *The Artist's Way at Work: Riding the Dragon* (William Morrow Paperbacks, 1999).

Chapter 10

48. https://sustainableninja.com/fashion-industry-waste-statistics/.

Chapter 11

49. https://www.formstack.com/blog/how-to-support-local-economy.

50. https://amiba.net/local-multiplier/.

51. https://sbecouncil.org/about-us/facts-and-data/.

52. https://en.wikipedia.org/wiki/Rochdale_Society_of_Equitable_Pioneers.

53. https://fossilfuel.com/why-banks-are-refusing-to-fund-fossil-fuels/.

54. https://www.bankbound.com/blog/why-bank-locally/.

55. https://theimpactinvestor.com/socially-responsible-banks/.

56. https://theimpactinvestor.com/green-credit-cards/.

57. https://www.ofn.org/cdfi-locator/.

58. https://bankforgood.org/.

Part Five Introduction

59. For a good description of commonly used tax-deferred saving instruments see https://www.investopedia.com/ask/answers/12/401k.asp.

60. For an excellent book on the topic of Self-Directed IRAs see Michael H. Shuman, *Put Your Money Where Your Life Is: How to Invest Locally Using Self-Directed IRAs and Solo 401(k)s* (California: Berret-Koehler, 2020).

61. Charles Eisenstein, *The More Beautiful World Our Hearts Know is Possible* (California: North Atlantic Books, 2013), 25.

62. Joyce Rupp and Macrina Wiederkehr, *Circle of Life*, (Notre Dame, IN, Soren Books, 2005). Reprinted with permission.

Chapter 12

63. https://www.investopedia.com/terms/c/conscious-capitalism.asp.

64. Conscious Capitalism, Inc. is a 501(C)(3) nonprofit corporation that catalyzes the larger Conscious Capitalism movement of business leaders changing the practice and perception of capitalism to elevate humanity. www.consciouscapitalism.org.

65. https://www.consciouscapitalism.org/philosophy.

66. https://www.un.org/sustainabledevelopment/takeaction/.

67. https://www.un.org/sustainabledevelopment/development-agenda/.

68. http://documents1.worldbank.org/curated/en/744701582827333101/pdf/Understanding-the-Cost-of-Achieving-the-Sustainable-Development-Goals.pdf, p. 4.

69. https://unglobalcompact.org/take-action/action/globalallianceforsdgfinance.

70. Homepage - https://www.angelsofimpact.com.

71. https://futurecrunch.com/.

Chapter 13

72. Charles Eisenstein, *Sacred Economics: Money Gift & Society in the Age of Transition* (Berkeley: Evolver Editions, 2011), 352.

73. Homepage - https://littlefreelibrary.org/.

74. https://www.investopedia.com/articles/insurance/090116/5-biggest-microfinance-companies-bbrijk.asp.

75. https://www.reportlinker.com/p05799111/Global-Microfinance-Industry.html?utm_source= GNW.

76. https://www.kiva.org/.

77. https://grameenfoundation.org/.

78. https://www.patreon.com/.

79. https://www.gofundme.com/.

80. https://www.indiegogo.com/.

81. https://www.mayoclinic.org/healthy-lifestyle/adult-health/in-depth/friendships/art-20044860.

82. https://orrgroup.com/giving-usas-2021-report-on-philanthropy-what-we-expected-what-surprised-us-and-what-the-findings-tell-us-about-the-future/.

83. https://givingusa.org/giving-usa-limited-data-tableau-visualization/.

84. https://commonsenseeconomics.com/wp-content/uploads/CSE_E_Reading-Brooks-Why_Giving_Matters.pdf, p.1.

Chapter 14

85. https://consumer.ftc.gov/articles/giving-charity.

86. https://en.wikipedia.org/wiki/The_Great_Wealth_Transfer_(United_States)

87. https://investforbetter.org/.

88. Online Courses - Learn Anything, On Your Schedule | Udemy / https://www.udemy.com.

89. https://www.coursera.org/.

90. https://www.linkedin.com/learning/.

91. https://greenmoney.com/.

92. Janine Firpo, *Activate Your Money: Invest to Grow Your Wealth and Build a Better World* (New Jersey: John Wiley and Sons, 2021), 32.

93. https://www.investopedia.com/terms/i/investing.asp.

94. https://www.morningstar.com/.

95. https://impactentrepreneur.com/five-questions-to-guide-esg-investors-when-vetting-companies/.

96. https://www.investopedia.com/terms/r/riskreturntradeoff.asp.

97. https://www.investopedia.com/terms/i/impact-investing.asp.

98. https://www.investopedia.com/articles/economics/08/protest-divestment-south-africa.asp.

99. https://www.investopedia.com/news/history-impact-investing/.

100. Brian Beckon, Amy Cortese, Janice Shade, Michael H. Shuman. *Community Investment Funds: A How-To Guide for Building Local Wealth, Equity and Justice*, A Publication of the National Coalition for Community Capital and The Solidago Foundation, 2021, 3.

101. Indranil Ghosh, *Powering Prosperity: A Citizens Guide to Shaping the 21st Century* (Bombardier Books, 2020), 236.

102. https://InvestWithValues.com.

103. https://www.thebalancemoney.com/questions-to-potential-financial-advisor-2388445.

Chapter 15

104. Mark Anielski, *An Economy of Well Being: Common Sense Tools for Building Genuine Wealth and Happiness* (Canada: New Society Publishers, 2018), 211.

Appendix 1

105. Julia Cameron, *The Vein of Gold: A Journey to Your Creative Heart* (New York: Penguin, 1996).

106. https://mindfulnessexercises.com/forgiveness-meditation/.

107. https://jackkornfield.com/forgiveness-meditation/.

108. https://www.thoughtfieldtherapy.net/.

109. https://balancedlifetaichi.com/blog/what-is-meridian-tapping.

110. https://www.emofree.com/eft-tutorial/tapping-basics/how-to-do-eft.html.

About the Author

Genevieve Chavez Mitchell is an author, a local activist, a global citizen, a conscious investor, and an artist. Genevieve's background includes raising four sons, business and non-profit consulting, natural health care, and portfolio management. She coauthored the book *Prayers to the Goddess: A Moon Cycle Devotion*, with Anne Key. She has been involved and participating in priestess study and work for many years. She and her husband manage their modest investment portfolio by investing in people and businesses that create a healthy, sustainable world. This is her work and a way to use her talents and resources to benefit her community.

Genevieve loves live music, being in nature, and her big, beautiful family. She's an avid photographer, and delights in hot mineral baths, good food, good friends, and good conversation. She is committed to a just, thriving, kind, regenerative Earth community. She lives in Albuquerque, New Mexico with her husband Paul.

She can be reached at genevievecmitchell.com

If you enjoyed reading *Sacred Money,* and purchased it through an online retailer, please return to the site and write a review to help others find the book.

www.ingramcontent.com/pod-product-compliance
Lightning Source LLC
LaVergne TN
LVHW010650110826
845149LV00014B/3017

* 9 7 8 1 9 6 1 3 4 7 1 9 9 *